Foreign Enterprise
in Developing
Countries

ISAIAH FRANK

Foreign Enterprise in Developing Countries

A Supplementary Paper
of the Committee for Economic
Development

THE JOHNS HOPKINS UNIVERSITY PRESS
BALTIMORE AND LONDON

Library of Congress Cataloging in Publication Data

Frank, Isaiah, 1917-
Foreign enterprise in developing countries.

(A Supplementary paper of the Committee for Economic Development)
Includes index.
1. Underdeveloped areas—International business
enterprises.   I. Title.
HD2755.5.F734   338.8'881724   79-3722
ISBN 0-8018-2343-9
ISBN 0-8018-2378-1 pbk.

FOREIGN ENTERPRISE IN DEVELOPING COUNTRIES
is sponsored by

Business and Social Research Institute (SNS), Sweden
Committee for Economic Development (CED), United States
Committee for Economic Development of Australia (CEDA)
European Committee for Social and Economic Progress
(CEPES), Germany
Institut de l'Entreprise (IDEP), France
Keizai Doyukai, Japan
Policy Studies Institute (PSI), Great Britain

Contents

ix

Preface

Multinational corporations, a major force in the world economy, have played a particularly significant role in the development of the countries of the Third World. For the past several decades, however, serious misgivings have been expressed by developing countries about the economic, social, and political consequences of the operations of multinationals. These concerns have engaged the attention of scholars, public officials, and international bodies all over the world and have inspired not only a vast literature but also a host of initiatives at the national and international levels designed to control the operations of multinational corporations.

This study, sponsored by the Committee for Economic Development (CED) and its counterpart organizations in other countries, is an attempt to probe the attitudes of multinationals on the main concerns about their operations expressed by developing countries. Based on in-depth interviews with ninety multinationals headquartered in the United States, Japan, Australia, and eight countries in Western Europe, the study is intended to contribute to improved public policies and more innovative company decision making. However, the views expressed in this study do not necessarily reflect those of the organizations that sponsored the project.

The results of the study have been discussed with experts and other representatives of Third World countries as background for the next stage of the project, the development of a policy statement by CED and possibly also by individual counterpart organizations that participated in the project.

ACKNOWLEDGMENTS

An international effort of this sort would have been impossible without the close cooperation of the participating organizations, the companies that agreed to be interviewed (Appendix A), and many individuals who collaborated or assisted at various stages of the project. To all of these, I am deeply grateful.

I want to express particular appreciation to Edmund B. Fitzgerald, CED Trustee and Chairman of the Subcommittee on Economic Relations between Industrial and Less Developed Countries, which had oversight responsibility for the project, and to Robert C. Holland, President of CED, for their steadfast encouragement, support, and valuable advice at every stage of the study. In addition, I wish to acknowledge the important role that Alfred C. Neal, former President of CED, played in the conception and original planning of the project.

Staff members of CED who have provided valuable cooperation include Frank Schiff, Chief Economist; Sol Hurwitz and Claudia Feurey, who had principal responsibility for publication; Kenneth Duberstein, who helped to expedite the financial support of the project; and Shirley Sherman and other CED staff members, who were always ready to lend a hand when they could be of assistance. I also wish to thank Patricia Murray, who edited the entire manuscript.

The results of the study owe much to the wholehearted cooperation of the directors of the counterpart organizations—Christian Allais (IDEP), Peter Grey (CEDA), Dr. Bernhard von Loeffelholz (CEPES), John Pinder (PSI), Bengt Ryden (SNS), and Seiichi Yamashita (Keizai Doyukai)—and to those individuals who, on behalf of the counterpart groups, conducted the interviews with the non-U.S.-based companies and wrote up the results: Emmanuel Jahan (IDEP), James Northcott (PSI), Professor Ehrenfried Pausenberger (CEPES), Dr. Marian Radetzki (SNS), Professor Ryo Hirono (Keizai Doyukai), and H. P. Anderson, A. Carroll, and P. Grey (CEDA).

The interviews with the U.S. companies were conducted by me, with the assistance of Mary Lindley, and by my Johns Hopkins colleagues in international economics, Professors Charles Pearson and James Riedel. The difficult job of synthesizing the interview responses for all the companies (contained in Part II of the study) was meticulously carried out by

Mary Lindley and Robert Fisher and, for a brief period, by Betsy Stillman.

The task of administering and coordinating this seven-country project proved far more complex than originally anticipated. Without the intelligent, conscientious, and cheerful help of my former and current research assistants, Mary Lindley and Robert Fisher, I cannot conceive of the many pieces having been pulled together and the project carried to completion. A great deal of credit is also due my secretary, Lucille Preston Burjorjee, for her unfailing willingness to cooperate in countless ways.

Thoughtful review and advice were provided at the various stages of the project by members of the CED Subcommittee. I wish to acknowledge particularly the valuable comments of Professor Anne O. Krueger of the University of Minnesota, who served as an advisor to the Subcommittee; of Franklin A. Lindsay, Chairman of CED's Research and Policy Committee; and of Professor Thomas C. Schelling of Harvard University, Chairman of CED's Research Advisory Board. Professor Raymond Vernon of Harvard University reviewed an early draft of the study and provided many helpful suggestions. Useful comments were also received from staff members of the United Nations Industrial Development Organization (UNIDO), who reviewed the project questionnaire, and of the United Nations Centre on Transnational Corporations (UNCTC), who provided an extensive critique of the draft study. All these individuals are, of course, absolved of any responsibility for statements made in the study.

Finally, my warm appreciation goes to Mme. Renée Coret, who served as a general assistant to Mr. Fitzgerald, Chairman of the CED Subcommittee, in connection with the various international meetings on the project. She assisted gallantly in arrangements and interpreting and also was responsible for translating the study into French.

Isaiah Frank

Part I

Background

ONE

Design and Purpose of the Project

Following the fourfold increase in oil prices by the Organization of Petroleum Exporting Countries (OPEC) in late 1973, the Committee for Economic Development (CED) and its counterpart organizations in Western Europe, Japan, and Australia[1] joined in a study of the implications of this momentous event for the world economy. That study resulted in a joint policy statement, *International Economic Conse quences of High-Priced Energy*, published in September 1975.

While the energy study was in progress, an increasingly sharp confrontation was taking place between poor and rich countries, stimulated in part by the OPEC action. OPEC's dramatic success in forcing a shift of world wealth and income from developed countries to an organized group of developing countries strengthened the Third World's perceptions of its capacity to achieve many long-sought economic goals in the world arena. Formal expression was given to Third World demands in the Declaration on the Establishment of a New International Economic Order, adopted at the Sixth Special Session of the United Nations in May 1974. In December of the same year, the General Assembly overwhelmingly endorsed the Charter of Economic Rights and Duties of States, a document on which the United Nations had been working for several years at the request of the developing countries.

[1] The six counterpart organizations are: the Committee for Economic Development of Australia (CEDA); Germany, European Committee for Social and Economic Progress (CEPES); France, Institut de l'Entreprise (IDEP); Japan, Keizai Doyukai; Great Britain, Policy Studies Institute (PSI) [formerly Political and Economic Planning (PEP)]; and Sweden, Business and Social Research Institute (SNS).

During 1975, the developing countries held a series of conferences at which they sought to reach a consensus on specific proposals for transforming the New International Economic Order into concrete proposals for reforming the rules and norms of the present international economic system. The proposals covered virtually every aspect of North-South economic relations, including trade, aid, foreign investment, transfer of technology, and the international monetary system.

It was in response to these events that CEPES, the German counterpart, proposed that, upon completion of the energy project, the seven organizations turn their attention to some important aspect of the North-South economic confrontation. Because the organizations were in a position to draw upon the experience of the business leadership of their respective countries, it was decided that they could make their most useful contribution by examining those aspects of the debate having to do with private foreign direct investment and the role of multinational corporations in the developing countries.

BACKGROUND

The role of private foreign direct investment in the development process has long been a subject of controversy. With the wave of independence movements and the struggles for social and economic transformation in the Third World after World War II, the debate grew in intensity and was characterized by sharp polarization.

One view was widely shared by governments and business groups in the industrial countries. In the early postwar period, the shortage of capital was regarded as the main constraint on development. The role of public capital in the form of bilateral and multilateral economic assistance was conceived as that of helping to finance the social infrastructure (transport, power, communications, and so on) as a precondition for attracting the vast untapped reservoir of private capital in the rich countries. Although private portfolio capital was looked upon with favor, prospects seemed dim for the revival of international capital markets after the financial disasters of the 1930s. Private foreign direct investment was therefore regarded as the greatest potential source of those resources—capital as well as entrepreneurship, technology, management, and marketing—lacking in developing countries. Third World countries were encouraged to provide a hospitable climate for foreign investment, not only through a minimum of regulation but often through such special inducements as tax holidays and subsidies.

The other view was a highly critical assessment of the impact of private foreign direct investment in the Third World. Among the prominent articulators of this view were Hans Singer and various economists of the United Nations Economic Commission for Latin America (ECLA) school, who wrote against the backdrop of the classical colonial or neo-colonial pattern, which had historically dominated foreign direct investment. According to this view, foreign direct investment in poor countries was basically an exploitative relationship. Such investment was largely concentrated in extractive industries, and therefore it provided only weak linkages backward and forward with the rest of a nation's economy. Moreover, it tended to reinforce a pattern of development that over the long run would trap the poor countries in their poverty because of the inevitable decline in the prices of exports of primary commodities as compared with the price of imports of manufactured goods. At the same time, rich countries would gain both from high financial returns to their investors and from a flow of cheap raw materials for their own industries.

Even today, when the pattern of foreign investment has become much more complex and differentiated, the view persists in some quarters that this relationship is basically harmful to the developing countries in terms of both its economic effects and its impact on their political, social, and cultural fabric. According to Dudley Seers, a distinguished British scholar of development and former director of the planning staff of the Ministry of Overseas Development, the most compelling need of the poor countries today is, not for more financial aid, but for "curbing the power of the transnational corporations."[2]

Fortunately, the old stereotypes and their modern versions are giving way on both sides to more reasoned and thoughtful views of the problems confronting developing countries and of the role of multinational corporations. The companies are more sensitive to the fears of developing countries about foreign domination of their economies. The United States itself experienced a wave of concern about OPEC economic domination in the wake of the fourfold oil price increase and massive investments of OPEC surpluses in U.S. assets. Numerous proposals were ad-

[2] Dudley Seers, "The New Meaning of Development," *International Development Review* 19, no. 3 (1977): 7.

vanced to curb the power of OPEC to take control of the U.S. economy. This experience, which was shared in varying degrees by other industrialized nations, has led to a greater capacity to empathize with the determination of other countries to control their own destinies. As a consequence, multinational corporations now tend to be less ideological and more pragmatic and flexible in their approach to operations in the developing world.

At the same time, despite the rhetoric still emanating at the political level, many developing countries have achieved greater self-confidence in their technical negotiations with multinationals and are far more conscious of their ability to shape events and negotiate from positions of greater strength.

In this atmosphere, the time seemed ripe to contribute to a better understanding of the problems and tensions that remain in this field by tapping the diverse and practical operating experience in the Third World of the companies represented in the membership of CED and its collaborating organizations. The objective was to obtain from the appropriate officers of the companies reactions to the main concerns about their operations expressed by developing countries and to solicit ideas for dealing with those problems in mutually advantageous ways. We thus hoped to clarify some important facts and issues as a basis for both more innovative company decision making and improved public policies at the national and international levels.

PROJECT DESIGN AND METHOD

The core of the project was to be in-depth interviews with parent companies based both in the countries represented by the participating organizations and in other nations. By including firms based in the different home countries, we hoped to acquire some information about, and understanding of, the similarity and diversity of approaches to the operations of transnational enterprises in the Third World. A total of ninety multinational companies were included: twenty-seven based in the United States, seventeen in Japan, thirteen in the United Kingdom, nine in Germany, seven in Sweden, seven in Australia, six in France, and one each in Belgium, Italy, Switzerland, and the Netherlands.[3]

In an effort to include a cross section of firms in the sample, a number

---

[3] See Appendix A for list of companies.

of criteria were applied: size of parent firm, industry group of parent firm, geographic distribution of subsidiaries in the developing world, size of host-country market as measured by GNP, stage of development of host country as measured by GNP per capita, and percentage of subsidiaries' equity owned by parent firm. These characteristics were considered particularly significant in conditioning the behavior and attitudes of multinationals with affiliates in the developing world.

Because substantial demands would be placed on participating firms in terms of senior executives' time and the provision of data, an effort was made to select firms represented in the membership of the collaborating organizations; it was presumed that such companies would be more inclined to devote the required resources to the project. But the need to obtain a sample that was broadly representative in terms of the aforementioned characteristics meant that some nonmember companies had to be included as well. In the final analysis, a major constraint in constructing the sample was the willingness of firms, whether or not they were members of the collaborating organizations, to be interviewed at length and to provide the factual data that were requested.

A firm agreeing to participate was asked initially to fill out a brief confidential factual questionnaire[4] on each of its subsidiaries in a developing country. The purpose of this questionnaire was to facilitate examination of the responses to the interview questions in relation to the location and type of subsidiaries controlled by each parent firm. However, not all parent firms complied with the request, either because of the difficulty of assembling the data from far-flung affiliates or because of hesitation to divulge private information even on a confidential basis. In a number of such cases, we turned to published material such as annual reports and (in the case of U.S. firms) 10-K forms for some of the relevant information. Factual questionnaires were filled out completely or in part for a total of 402 subsidiaries: 188 of U.S. companies, 84 of Japanese firms, 41 of Swedish firms, 41 of Australian firms, 31 of French companies, 7 of British companies, and 5 each of the Belgian and Italian firms.

The interview with senior executives of the parent firms, which was to be the heart of the study, was based on a questionnaire[5] consisting of forty-eight questions, many with multiple parts, designed to elicit reac-

[4] This questionnaire is reproduced in Appendix B.

[5] This questionnaire is reproduced in Appendix C.

tions to the principal concerns expressed by the developing countries about the operations of multinationals. In order to ensure coverage of the main problems as perceived by the developing countries, drafts of the questionnaire had been informally reviewed in advance by individuals in close touch with the developing countries on transnational corporation issues through their work as staff members of the United Nations Industrial Development Organization (UNIDO) and the United Nations Centre on Transnational Corporations.[6]

Through these interviews, we sought to obtain candid opinions and attitudes based on the actual experience of knowledgeable executives with responsibility for operations of affiliates in the Third World. This point was emphasized orally or in the letters of invitation in which, in addition to assuring the confidentiality of the replies, it was explicitly stated that we were not seeking official company views. Insofar as possible, we hoped to discourage formal responses prepared or vetted by companies' public information or legal departments. We believe that these efforts to ensure frankness and openness were successful, but of course, we cannot guarantee that 100 percent candor was achieved.

The interview questionnaire was sent to the companies well in advance in order to allow the executives ample time to think about the subjects raised and to plan for the presence of the appropriate people at the interview.[7]

One of the more difficult problems in working out the arrangements was the frequent need to interview people with different backgrounds and experience in the same company. Many of the individuals concerned did a great deal of traveling in conjunction with their responsibilities for foreign operations, and it took a lot of coordination to bring them and the interviewer together at the same time. The average number of company participants was three. But in the case of the American companies, for example, as many as thirteen people from the same firm participated in a single interview. The average length of the interviews was slightly more than four hours.

---

[6] Neither of these organizations should be presumed to bear any responsibility for the questionnaire or any other aspect of the project.

[7] There were two exceptions to this procedure. In the case of the Japanese firms only, written responses to the questionnaire were requested; interviews were then conducted to complement or clarify points in the written replies. Only a minority of the British companies received the questionnaire itself in advance. Instead, most of the firms were sent a note listing the main topics for discussion.

The interviews were carried out over a three-year period from mid-1976 to mid-1979; most were conducted during 1978.

Each collaborating organization prepared a summary of the responses of all its participating firms to each interview question. These summaries and the reports on the individual interviews were sent to CED for analysis and synthesis. The results are presented in Part II.

TWO

Foreign Enterprise in Developing Countries: Scope and Trends

Broadly speaking, a multinational corporation is a company that operates in several foreign countries through affiliates that are subject to some degree of central control. The parent company's influence may be exercised in a wide variety of ways, including control over such strategic aspects of the affiliate's operations as pricing policies, choice of technology, appointment of key personnel, and determination of markets.

The United Nations tends to favor the term *transnational* rather than *multinational* on the grounds that the former is more descriptive of the concept of a parent firm based in one country with operating affiliates in a number of foreign countries. The term *multinational* would then denote a company owned by several nationalities, whether or not it had affiliates in other countries. Actually, the preference for *transnational* is not merely technical; it also rests on the belief that the term more accurately reflects the quality of "domination" inherent in the parent-subsidiary relationship in contrast with the implication of coequality in *multinational*. Despite these distinctions, the words are used interchangeably in this study.

LIMITATIONS OF THE DATA BASE

Multinational corporations are responsible for most private foreign direct investment. But the measure of such investment is more limited than the total flow of resources from multinational enterprises. Private direct investment is generally understood to refer to the flow of equity and loan capital from parent to affiliate. But even in this limited sense of the flow of financial resources (including reinvested earnings), the measure understates the size of flows for which the parent is responsible. For example, a loan to a foreign affiliate from a home-country (or third-country) bank would not be included in foreign direct investment, even though the transaction may depend on the reputation or formal guarantee of the parent company.

A more important limitation is the fact that foreign direct investment does not necessarily reflect the flow of other resources—technology, management services, marketing services—from parent to affiliate. An increasing proportion of the activities of transnational enterprises in developing countries takes forms that are unrelated to financial flows from parents to subsidiaries but that nevertheless imply some degree of control by the foreign company. In the light of these trends, the conventional measures of foreign direct investment flows and stocks must be viewed as minimum indicators of the scope of the activities of multinational corporations.

Apart from this fundamental limitation of the data base, two other problems arise in attempting to measure direct investment originating not simply in one country but in the developed countries as a group. The first concerns the criterion for determining what constitutes private direct investment as opposed to portfolio investment. Because some measure of central control by the parent company is an essential part of the definition of direct investment, the problem is to give quantitative expression to this condition in terms of the required minimum percentage of equity ownership. The United States, Germany, and Sweden apply the standard of at least 10 percent; France, 20 percent; Australia, 25 percent. In the cases of the United Kingdom and Japan, strictly defined percentages are apparently not applied. Of course, any fixed threshold for equity is arbitrary, but the lack of uniformity of practice among home countries compounds the problem of aggregation.

The second problem in combining national data is the distortions inherent in converting the data into a single currency under conditions of inflation and fluctuating exchange rates of the type experienced during the last few years. Aggregates in terms of the U.S. dollar are seriously affected by changes in the value of the dollar relative to the currencies of other investor countries. For example, in mid-May 1978, the German mark had appreciated 72.6 percent in terms of the dollar, compared

Table 1. Net Flow [a] of Financial Resources to Developing Countries from Industrial Countries,[b] 1960 to 1978 (millions of dollars)

	Average, 1960–1965	Average, 1966–1971	1972	1973	1974	1975	1976	1977	1978
Official development assistance	$5,494	$ 6,663	$ 8,538	$ 9,378	$11,317	$13,585	$13,734	$14,696	$18,308
Other official flows	379	773	1,546	2,463	2,183	3,024	3,296	3,319	(4,000)
Private flows	3,186	6,020	8,333	9,458	7,330	22,152	20,872	29,988	(32,820)
Direct investment	1,789	2,902	4,234	4,719	1,124	10,494	7,824	8,792	(9,470)
Bilateral portfolio	536	818	1,984	3,286	3,795	5,313	5,166	10,454	(11,350)
Multilateral portfolio	201	513	667	257	-70	2,278	3,059	2,642	(2,000)
Export credits	660	1,794	1,448	1,196	2,481	4,067	4,823	8,100	(10,000)
Grants by private voluntary agencies	NA	NA	1,036	1,364	1,217	1,342	1,357	1,489	(1,500)
Total net flow [c]	$9,059	$13,456	$19,453	$22,663	$22,047	$40,103	$39,260	$49,492	($56,628)

SOURCES: Organization for Economic Cooperation and Development, *Development Assistance*, 1961-1971 issues; Organization for Economic Cooperation and Development, *Development Cooperation*, 1972-1978 issues. Figures for 1978 are from OECD *Press Release*, June 19, 1979. Figures slightly modified to reflect World Bank data.

NA = Not available.

( ) = Parentheses denote estimates.

[a] Gross disbursements less amortization receipts on earlier lending. The figures include flows to multilateral organizations.

[b] The countries include Australia, Austria, Belgium, Canada, Denmark, France, Germany, Italy, Japan, the Netherlands, New Zealand, Norway, Sweden, Switzerland, the United Kingdom, and the United States. Also included is the Commission of the European Economic Community.

[c] Figures prior to 1972 exclude New Zealand.

with its pre-June 1970 parity. Expressed in dollars, therefore, the book value of the total stock of U.S. and German direct investment abroad would have increased even if no new net flows had taken place over the period. Moreover, German investment would have risen substantially in proportion to U.S. investment. Because aggregate data on foreign investment are generally expressed in dollars, distorting effects of exchange rate changes should be kept in mind.

Finally, the U.S. government publishes comprehensive data on private direct investment in the developing countries; data for investment originating in other home countries are generally not available in the same detail or in comparable forms. Nevertheless, the brief quantitative review that follows attempts, insofar as possible, to present a consistent picture of the scope and trends of private direct investment in the Third World originating in all developed countries. It is based mainly on Organization for Economic Cooperation and Development (OECD) and U.N. sources in which efforts have been made to achieve comparability of foreign investment data supplied by different countries.

SIZE AND TRENDS

Between 1972 and 1978, private direct investment flows to developing countries averaged $6,665 million, or just under 19 percent of the total of such flows to all destinations. About 40 percent of the flows in 1976 were accounted for by reinvested earnings.[1]

Share of Private Direct Investment in Capital Flows

The changing quantitative role of private foreign direct investment in the total flow of financial resources to the Third World is shown in detail in Table 1 and is summarized in Table 2. Private direct investment as a proportion of the total flows from the industrial countries was 19.7 percent between 1960 and 1965, 21.6 percent between 1966 and 1971, and 18.7 percent between 1972 and 1978.

In recent years, however, the share of direct investment in total private flows to developing countries has substantially declined because of the greatly stepped-up role of long-term lending by international banks (see "Private flows, bilateral portfolio" in Table 1). Not surprisingly,

[1] United Nations, *Transnational Corporations in World Development: A Reexamination* (New York: United Nations, 1978), p. 58.

Table 2. Share of Private Direct Investment in Total Private Flow and Total
Net Flow of Financial Resources to Developing Countries

Private Direct Investment as a Percentage of:	*1960–1965*	*1966–1971*	*1972–1978*
Total private flow	56.2	48.2	35.6
Total net flow	19.7	21.6	18.7

SOURCE: Table 1.

the same developing countries that most attract direct investment from multinational corporations (Brazil and Mexico) are also the ones that have borrowed most on international capital markets. As countries move up the development scale, their potential sources of external finance naturally increase.

Changing Origin of Private Direct Investment

According to Table 3, the stock of private foreign investment in developing countries more than doubled between 1967 and 1977, amounting to over $85 billion by the end of 1977. The extent of the real increase is inflated by both price increases and the depreciation of the dollar in relation to the currencies of the other major investing countries, but because the stock data are in terms of book value, a substantial increase has undoubtedly occurred. The most dramatic increases in shares that partly reflect such rate changes were those of Japan, which rose from 2.0 to 6.7 percent of the total, and Germany, which rose from 3.4 to 8.0 percent. However, stock of U.S. origin was slightly less than 47 percent in 1977, compared with almost 50 percent at the end of 1967. The next most substantial declines were registered by the United Kingdom and France, with the U.K. decline being partly attributable to the depreciation of sterling in relation to the dollar over this period. Although both Australia and Sweden gained in shares, each still accounted for only about 1 percent of the total stock of private foreign direct investment at the end of 1977.

The varying roles played by different countries of origin in particular host countries is shown in Table 4. For example, although the United States is the largest single source of direct investment in Brazil, its share has been declining. Germany, the Netherlands, Sweden, Japan, and Switzerland have increased their shares in recent years. Taken together, the direct investment stake of these five countries exceeded that of the

Table 3. Estimated Book Value of Stocks (Year-end 1967 and Year-end 1977) and
Flows (1968–1972 and 1973–1977) of Private Foreign Direct Investment in Developing Countries (millions of dollars)

	Stock, Year-end 1967	Flow, 1968–1972	Flow, 1973–1977	Stock, Year-end 1977	Stock, Year-end 1967 (percent)	Flow, 1968–1972 (percent)	Flow, 1973–1977 (percent)	Stock, Year-end 1977 (percent)
Australia	$ 101	$ 354	$ 428	$ 883	0.3	2.1	1.3	1.0
Austria	7	12	71	90	—a	0.1	0.2	0.1
Belgium	692	160	378	1,230	2.0	0.9	1.1	1.4
Canada	1,477	433	1,438	3,348	4.2	2.5	4.4	3.9
Denmark	31	49	102	182	0.1	0.3	0.3	0.2
France	2,980	1,253	1,310	5,543	8.5	7.3	4.0	6.5
Germany	1,198	1,703	3,915	6,816	3.4	10.0	11.9	8.0
Italy	879	860	871	2,610	2.5	5.0	2.6	3.1
Japan	702	923	4,037	5,662	2.0	5.4	12.3	6.7
Netherlands	1,789	889	1,291	3,969	5.1	5.2	3.9	4.7
Norway	12	52	105	169	—a	0.3	0.3	0.2
Sweden	189	198	404	791	0.5	1.2	1.2	0.9
Switzerland	695	321	854	1,870	2.0	1.9	2.6	2.2
United Kingdom	6,804	1,535	3,779	12,118	19.4	9.0	11.5	14.2
United States	17,448	8,369	13,949	39,766	49.8	48.9	42.4	46.8
Total	$35,004	$17,111	$32,932	$85,047	100.0	100.0	100.0	100.0

SOURCES: Organization for Economic Cooperation and Development, Stock of Private Direct Investments by DAC Countries in Developing Countries, End 1967 (Paris: Organization for Economic Cooperation and Development, 1972); Organization for Economic Cooperation and Development, Development Cooperation, 1971–1978 issues.

a Negligible or less than 0.1 percent

Table 4. Stock of Direct Investment in Selected Developing Countries and Territories, by Country of Origin, Selected Years

Country, Territory, or Area of Origin	Argentina	Brazil		Colombia [a]		Mexico		Panama	
	Latin America								
	1973	1971	1976	1971	1975	1971	1975	1969	1974
Total value of stock (millions of dollars)	$2,274	$2,911	$9,005	$503	$632	$2,997	$4,736	$214	$534
Distribution of stock (percent)									
United States	39.5	37.7	32.2	55.9	48.1	80.9	68.7	90.8	86.3
Canada	3.9	10.1	5.3	10.1	10.1	1.7	2.3	NA	NA
Western Europe									
France	8.5	4.5	3.6	3.4	4.3	1.7	1.0	NA	NA
Germany, Federal Republic of	4.5	11.4	12.4	2.4	2.5	2.8	2.3	NA	NA
Italy	1.1	1.1	0.9	NA	NA	1.6	0.5	NA	NA
Netherlands	6.3	1.2	2.6	3.0	3.5	1.1	2.3	NA	NA
Spain	0.4	NS	NS	NA	NA	0.8	0.1	NA	NA
Sweden	2.0	2.0	2.4	NA	NA	1.2	1.1	NA	NA
Switzerland	9.1	6.6	10.9	2.8	4.6	2.8	3.0	2.5	2.3
United Kingdom	12.0	9.4	4.7	2.0	2.2	3.0	5.6	2.6	3.2
Japan	0.3	4.3	11.2	0.1	0.6	0.7	1.3	NA	NA
Other countries									
Argentina	NS	0.3	0.2	NA	NA	NA	NA	NA	NA
Brazil	0.4	NS	NS	0.1	0.3	NA	NA	NA	NA
Panama	3.5	2.8	3.1	7.2	8.3	NS	2.5	NS	NS
Venezuela	NS	0.1	0.1	2.0	3.0	0.2	NA	NA	NA
All other [b]	8.2	8.7	10.4	13.0	12.5	1.7	9.3	4.0	8.1
Total	100.0	100.0	100.0	100.0	100.0	100.0	100.0	100.0	100.0

Asia

	Hong Kong		India	Indonesia[c]		Korea, Republic of		Philippines		Singapore[d]		Thailand[e]	
	1971	1976	1974	1971	1976	1973	1975	1973	1976	1971	1976	1969	1975
Total value of stock (millions of dollars)	$759	$1,952	$1,683	$1,831	$6,362	$582	$927	$146	$513	$543	$1,523	$70	$175
Distribution of stock (percent)													
United States	53.5	47.2	12.3	25.2	6.7	21.5	17.4	64.2	47.9	31.8	32.9	26.5	14.0
Canada	NA	NA	6.2	NA	NA	NA	NA	0.3	7.8	NA	NA	NA	NA
Western Europe													
France	NA	1.2	NA	NA	NA	0.6	0.6	NA	NA	NA	NA		
Germany, Federal Republic of	0.8	1.0	3.5	0.9	2.7	0.7	0.6	0.2	0.3	1.3	3.0		
Italy	NA	NA	NA	NA	NA	0.2	NA	NA	NA	NA	NA		
Netherlands	2.3	1.2	3.0	2.0	2.5	1.1	6.2	NA	NA	17.5	14.0	11.9[f]	5.8[f]
Sweden	NA	NA	3.5	NA	NA	NA	NA	NA	NA	NA	NA		
Switzerland	1.8	2.2	5.5	NA	NA	NA	NA	0.8	1.8	NA	NA		
United Kingdom	11.3	8.2	60.8	NA	NA	NA	NA	16.4	5.8	18.6	14.8	4.7	2.0
Japan	22.4	15.4	2.0	29.7	36.9	70.7	66.5	9.7	24.2	6.8	14.0	36.6	41.0
Australia	4.5	5.2	NA	5.0	2.6	NA	NA	0.3	2.5	NA	NA	1.0	0.3
Other countries and territories													
Hong Kong	NS	NS	NA	6.3	10.3	0.8	0.6	1.3	1.8	NA	NA	NA	NA
Korea, Republic of	NA	NA	NA	2.8	0.9	NS	NS	NA	NA	NA	NA	NA	NA
Philippines	0.3	0.3	NA	14.3	4.2	NA	NA	NS	NS	NA	NA	0.3	0.8
Singapore	1.1	3.1	NA	2.6	1.8	NA	NA	NA	NA	NS	NS	NA	NA
Thailand	0.3	7.0	NA	NA	NA	NA	NA	NA	NA	NA	NA	NS	NS
Bahamas	NA	NA	0.6	NA	NA	NA	NA	NA	NA	NA	NA	NA	NA
Panama	NA	NA	1.4	NA	NA	0.9	2.5	0.2	0.4	NA	NA	NA	NA
All other[b]	1.1	3.5	3.4	11.0	31.4	3.5	5.4	6.6	7.5	23.9	21.0	4.4	14.7
Total	100.0	100.0	100.0	100.0	100.0	100.0	100.0	100.0	100.0	100.0	100.0	100.0	100.0

Table 4 *(continued)*

| | Africa | |
| | Nigeria | |
	1968	*1973*
Total value of stock		
(millions of dollars)	$999	$1,999
Distribution of stock		
(percent)		
United States	19.8	29.2
Western Europe		
(excluding United		
Kingdom)	18.9	19.6
United Kingdom	56.3	44.2
All other[b]	5.9	7.0
Total	100.0	100.0

SOURCE: United Nations, *Transnational Corporations in World Development: A Reexamination* (New York: United Nations, 1978), Annex III, Table III-49, pp. 256–258.

NA = Not available.
NS = Not significant.
[a] Excludes investment in the petroleum sector.
[b] Includes developed and developing countries of origin for which no separate data are available.
[c] Approved projects.
[d] Investment in manufacturing only.
[e] Registered capital of foreign firms.
[f] This figure represents the total stock for all Western European countries, including those not listed in the table.

United States in 1976. However, interpretation of this development must take into account the distorting effect of the appreciation in the dollar value of the currencies of these countries between 1971 and 1976.

The preponderance of Japanese direct investment in such Asian countries as Korea, Thailand, and Indonesia is comparable to that of U.S. investment in Latin American countries. But whereas the U.S. investment share in most countries of Latin America is diminishing (although the absolute amounts continue to increase), the Japanese share in most Asian countries is increasing. In India, however, the United Kingdom remains the major investor country.

Investment Distribution by Host Country

The regional distribution of foreign investment by recipient developing countries is presented in Table 5. Latin America emerges as the dominant recipient region, accounting for 37 percent of total flows between

1969 and 1976 and for 45 percent of the stock of foreign investment at the end of that period. (The prominence of Latin America is even greater in the stock of U.S. foreign direct investment. Latin American countries accounted for almost 60 percent of such stock in 1976.)[2] Brazil is by far the largest single recipient among the developing countries (15.8 percent), no other having attracted even half that volume. The other major recipients (excluding the countries of southern Europe) are Mexico, Indonesia, Venezuela, and Nigeria.

Interestingly, the entire Middle East accounted at the end of 1976 for only $4.1 billion of the stock of foreign direct investment in developing nations (5.6 percent of the total), an amount less than half that invested in Brazil alone. This pattern reflects, in part, the disinvestment in petroleum that has taken place in recent years as oil-producing countries have increasingly nationalized their foreign-owned facilities.

SECTORAL SHIFTS

The changing pattern and trends in the sectoral distribution of direct foreign investment in developing countries is shown in Table 6. A comparison of the percentages for stocks and flows conveys a sense of shifts in the pattern of investment between 1965 and 1972. For example, investment in petroleum remained a steady one-third of the total, but a clear shift in the flow of petroleum investment away from Latin America, especially in favor of Africa, took place. The stock of investment in manufacturing also constituted about one-third of the total, but the trend in its share rose in every region of the developing world. In contrast, the share of investment in mining declined and constituted less than 10 percent of the total at the end of 1972.

The relative decline of foreign direct investment in mining ventures in developing countries is also illustrated by data on mining companies' allocations of exploration expenditures (see Table 7). Despite the richer ore bodies in the developing countries, there has been an increasing concentration of exploration expenditures in the developed countries. It is impossible to say, however, how much of this trend reflects the avoidance by multinationals of Third World mineral development because of

[2] Obie G. Whichard, "U.S. Direct Investment in 1976," *Survey of Current Business,* U.S. Department of Commerce, August 1977, p. 45.

Table 5. Regional Distribution of Private Foreign Direct Investment Flows (Net, 1969-1976) and
Estimated Stock (Year-end 1976) from Industrial Countries[a] to Developing Countries, by Selected Recipient Countries[b]

	Flows (millions of U.S. dollars)										Stock (millions of U.S. dollars)	Percent of Total[c]
	1969	1970	1971	1972	1973	1974	1975	1976	1969–76	Percent of Total[c]		
Europe	168	303	224	424	652	895	810	369	3,845	8.8	6,745	9.2
Greece	5	10	9	14	88	143	43	46	348	0.8	946	1.3
Spain	105	240	127	366	509	668	578	235	2,828	6.5	4,605	6.3
Turkey	-1	4	1	1	26	24	47	-5	97	0.2	495	0.7
Africa	635	802	587	656	202	275	948	928	5,033	11.5	11,629	15.9
Algeria	85	80	1	41	40	8	29	44	328	0.8	394	0.5
Libya	152	283	104	151	-193	-3	-576	263	181	0.4	893	1.2
Morocco	—[d]	5	4	7	5	-26	5	1	1	—	301	0.4
Angola	4	2	2	2	8	7	—	-1	24	0.1	99	0.1
Zaire	15	6	6	10	18	52	9	238	354	0.8	1,088	1.5
Gabon	—	1	—	—	11	13	47	7	78	0.2	627	0.9
Ghana	22	7	-4	6	8	14	7	-2	58	0.1	298	0.4
Ivory Coast	1	-3	—	-1	4	1	6	30	38	0.1	450	0.6
Liberia	-2	73	-36	23	78	57	180	83	456	1.0	883	1.2
Nigeria	66	61	48	76	71	88	472	-152	730	1.7	2,748	3.8
Rhodesia	23	19	22	23	30	33	25	—	175	0.4	300	0.4
Zambia	9	10	8	22	17	14	32	-1	113	0.3	201	0.3
Latin America and Caribbean	1,195	1,510	1,391	1,558	3,207	4,677	4,307	2,846	20,691	36.7	40,027	(44.8)
	(1,185)[e]	(1,441)	(1,514)	(1,463)	(2,629)	(2,668)	(3,365)	(1,756)	(16,021)		(32,787)	
Jamaica	-3	1	13	-7	5	3	32	-79	-36	-0.1	891	1.2
Mexico	196	137	79	181	252	480	393	-166	1,552	3.6	4,634	6.3
Panama	154	195	221	18	222	14	340	128	1,292	3.0	2,378	3.3
Trinidad and Tobago	2	7	-3	6	-7	10	3	1	19	—	1,201	1.6
West Indies	37	14	17	27	25	110	1	4	235	0.5	744	1.0
Argentina	114	84	123	70	92	35	54	210	782	1.8	2,210	3.0
Brazil	225	294	371	629	1,257	1,307	1,457	1,366	6,906	15.8	10,466	14.3
Chile	-80	-29	-24	-102	-10	-43	-128	4	-412	-0.9	404	0.6
Colombia	53	4	72	-7	12	38	49	6	227	0.5	1,206	1.6
Peru	35	-9	11	45	87	457	327	159	1,112	2.5	1,859	2.5

									%		%
Middle East	106	-67	169	466	878	-314	1,536	1,109	3,863	8.9	4,090	5.6
Iran	40	15	23	4	36	-614	495	-109	-110	-0.3	1,091	1.5
Iraq	—	-1	—	—	-7	-9	-45	1	-61	-0.1	121	0.2
Kuwait	41	26	—	—	—	—	—	-1	66	0.2	649	0.9
Saudi Arabia	4	7	8	4	1	6	32	44	106	0.2	694	0.9
Asia and Oceania	551	779	912	855	1,813	1,699	3,382	1,780	11,771	(26.9)	17,891	(24.5)
				(1,810)ᵉ	(1,697)	(3,379)	(1,770)	(11,753)		(17,881)	
India	40	42	47	19	41	52	85	19	345	0.8	2,419	3.3
Pakistan	5	4	—	-1	—	—	6	-1	13	—	749	1.0
Hong Kong	23	26	31	58	143	81	215	79	633	1.5	1,379	1.9
Indonesia	48	49	117	90	348	182	1,289	746	2,869	6.6	4,246	5.8
Republic of Korea	5	14	32	67	261	81	51	83	594	1.4	1,033	1.4
Malaysia	6	37	32	65	139	123	73	51	526	1.2	2,351	3.2
Philippines	70	-3	17	14	60	140	117	152	567	1.3	1,372	1.9
Singapore	9	16	22	46	105	92	70	42	402	0.9	1,742	2.4
Thailand	17	14	8	21	20	44	19	16	159	0.4	346	0.5
Papua New Guinea	42	130	47	86	112	73	-2	49	537	1.2	749	1.0
Total ᶠ	2,919	3,544	3,633	4,474	6,717	7,874	11,506	7,649	48,316		80,382	
Tax-haven countries ᵍ	10	69	-123	95	581	2,011	945	1,100	4,688		7,250	
Total ᶜ	**2,909**	**3,475**	**3,756**	**4,379**	**6,136**	**5,863**	**10,561**	**6,549**	**43,628**	**100.0**	**73,132**	**100.0**

SOURCE: K. Billerbeck and Y. Yasugi, *Private Direct Investment in Developing Countries*, World Bank Staff Paper no. 348 (Washington D.C.: International Bank for Reconstruction and Development, July 1979), p. 70.

NOTES: 1. The data in this table for the years 1973 and 1974 are not consistent with those on total private direct investment in Table 1 because this table does not reflect major recomputations of the U.S. data for the years that are reflected in revised OECD data, including those in Table 1.

2. Items may not add to totals because of rounding and incomplete country listing.

ᵃ See Table 1, note b, for list of countries.
ᵇ Includes reinvested earnings.
ᶜ Excludes tax-haven countries.
ᵈ Flows of less than ± $500,000.
ᵉ Figures in parentheses are those excluding tax-haven countries.
ᶠ Includes unspecified total.
ᵍ Bahamas, Bermuda, Netherland Antilles, and New Hebrides.

increased political risk and how much reflects primarily a shift toward the use of state enterprises in the developing countries for exploration on the basis of technical and service contracts between governments and multinationals.

PATTERNS OF OWNERSHIP

Foreign ownership patterns in manufacturing affiliates in the developing countries differ markedly among transnational firms based in different home countries. As the data in Table 8 demonstrate, affiliates of

Table 6. Regional and Sectoral Distribution of Estimated Stock (Year-end 1972) and Flows (1965–1972) of Private Foreign Direct Investment in Developing Countries (percent)

	Petroleum		Mining		Manufacturing		Other		Total	
	Stocks	Flows	Stocks	Flows	Stocks	Flows	Stocks	Flows	Stocks	Flows
Europe[a]	0.8	1.0	0.2	0.2	4.4	6.2	1.9	3.4	7.4	10.8
Africa	8.6	12.5	3.2	2.4	3.4	3.5	4.0	3.3	19.2	21.7
Latin America and Caribbean	11.2	4.7	4.6	2.6	18.8	20.2	13.1	10.2	47.7	37.7
Middle East	7.6	8.0	—	—	0.6	0.7	0.4	0.7	8.6	9.4
Asia and Oceania	5.1	7.1	1.3	2.4	5.3	6.7	5.5	4.2	17.1	20.4
Total	33.3	33.3	9.3	7.6	32.5	37.3	24.9	21.8	100.0	100.0

SOURCES: Organization for Economic Cooperation and Development, *Development Cooperation,* 1973 issue; Organization for Economic Cooperation and Development, *Planning, Income Distribution, Private Foreign Investment* (Paris: OECD Development Centre, 1974).
[a] OECD data on private foreign investment includes eight low-income countries in this category: Cyprus, Gibraltar, Greece, Malta, Portugal, Spain, Turkey, and Yugoslavia.

Table 7. Allocation of Exploration Expenditures in the Mining Industry, by Country Group, 1961 to 1975 (percent)

Country Group	1961–1965	1966–1970	1971–1975
Developing countries	34.6	30.0	14.4
Developed countries	65.4	70.0	85.6
Total	100.0	100.0	100.0

SOURCE: H. Brownrigg, "Stabilizing the Political Risk Environment in the International Mining Industry," London Business School, 1977, as cited in United Nations, *Transnational Corporations in World Development: A Reexamination* (New York: United Nations, 1978), p. 67.

Table 8. Distribution of Ownership Patterns[a] of 1,276 Manufacturing Affiliates[b] of 391 Transnational Corporations Established in Developing Countries, by Period of Establishment, 1951 to 1975 (percent)

Home Country and Type of Ownership	Number Established as Percent of Total				
	Before 1951	1951–1960	1961–1965	1966–1970	1971–1975
Affiliates of 180 U.S.-based corporations					
Wholly owned	58.4	44.5	37.4	46.2	43.7
Majority owned	12.2	21.4	19.2	17.8	17.3
Co-owned	5.6	7.9	11.4	11.2	10.4
Minority owned	11.2	18.8	21.7	21.5	28.1
Unknown	12.6	7.4	10.3	3.3	0.4
Total	100.0	100.0	100.0	100.0	100.0
Affiliates of 135 European- and U.K.-based corporations					
Wholly owned	39.1	31.6	20.9	18.9	—
Majority owned	15.4	20.1	15.6	16.4	—
Co-owned	5.3	6.6	11.1	6.6	—
Minority owned	9.8	27.9	35.8	42.1	—
Unknown	30.5	13.9	16.6	16.0	—
Total	100.0	100.0	100.0	100.0	—
Affiliates of 76 other transnational corporations[c]					
Wholly owned	27.4	16.7	10.7	6.1	—
Majority owned	8.2	26.2	12.6	8.2	—
Co-owned	12.3	7.1	6.3	7.5	—
Minority owned	16.4	42.9	66.7	74.2	—
Unknown	35.6	7.1	3.8	3.9	—
Total	100.0	100.0	100.0	100.0	—

SOURCES: United Nations, *Transnational Corporations in World Development: A Reexamination* (New York: United Nations, 1978), Table III-25, p. 229, and data supplied by the Harvard Multinational Enterprise Project.

[a] Affiliates of which the parent firm of the system owns 95 percent or more are classified as wholly owned; over 50 percent, as majority owned; equal percentages, as co-owned; 5 to under 50 percent, as minority owned.

[b] The affiliates of U.S.-based corporations are those in which the U.S.-based parent of the multinational enterprise held a direct equity interest; the affiliates of corporations based in the United Kingdom, Western Europe, and Japan include those in which parent companies held equity interest indirectly through other affiliates.

[c] Of these 76 corporations, 61 are based in Japan.

U.S.-based companies are predominantly wholly owned. Although this predominance has persisted since the early 1950s, a clear trend toward an increasing proportion of minority-owned U.S. affiliates is discernible. (A minority-owned affiliate is one in which the parent company owns less than 50 percent of the equity.) In the case of European-based affiliates, minority ownership has become the most common form, accounting for more than 40 percent of all newly established affiliates in the period from 1966 to 1970. However, the most striking trend toward minority ownership by foreign companies is evidenced among Japanese-based affiliates, where the proportion has grown from 16 percent before 1951 to 74 percent in the 1966–1970 period. This major shift can be explained in part by the heavy concentration of Japan's activities in extractive industries. In such cases, host developing countries often insist on domestic majority ownership. Furthermore, Japan is sensitive to its postwar image in the formerly occupied areas of eastern and southern Asia.

FLOWS OF TECHNOLOGY AND MANAGEMENT

Resources flow to affiliates of multinational firms not only in the form of capital but also in other forms, especially technology and management. But it is no simple matter, either conceptually or statistically, to disentangle these various flows of services. An investment that finances the importation of capital goods by an affiliated company is at the same time contributing to the stocks of capital and technology because some new technology is almost invariably embodied in capital equipment. More broadly, the typical pattern of foreign direct investment is to supply capital and disembodied technological and managerial services in a single package in the form of know-how. Some of the services of such technology and management are often paid for separately through royalties and fees. But host governments do not always permit such payments, especially to parents of wholly owned affiliates. In those cases, the compensation for technological and managerial services is, in effect, included in profits and appears in the statistics as earnings on capital rather than as royalties and fees.

With these qualifications in mind, it is possible to attempt a comparison between the flow of the services of capital and the flow of separate technological and managerial services by comparing income payments to parents of affiliates in developing countries and payments of royalties and fees. Income payments in 1974 amounted to $16,400 million; royalties and fees in 1975 were estimated at $1,100 million.[3] However, the bulk of the income payments ($13,600 million) was from oil-producing countries; whereas more than half of the royalties and fees came from Latin America, especially the larger, more developed countries such as Brazil and Mexico, in which manufacturing investment predominated.

Two inferences can reasonably be drawn from these data: First, a substantial portion of the income payments from affiliates in oil-producing countries is probably a proxy for what would appear as royalties and fees in other countries. Second, the use of aggregate data for comparing these various flows is highly deceptive because of wide divergencies in host-country law and regulations and in the practices of multinationals with respect to the allocation of payments to earnings on capital or to royalties and fees.

SUMMARY

The data base for stocks and flows of private foreign investment is subject to substantial conceptual and measurement limitations. In recent years, these have been aggravated by the distortions inherent in converting national data into dollars under conditions of inflation and flexible exchange rates.

Between 1972 and 1978, private direct investment flows to developing countries averaged $6.7 billion annually. As a proportion of the total flow of financial resources from OECD countries to the Third World, private direct investment was 19.7 percent between 1960 and 1965 and 18.7 percent between 1972 and 1978. It has declined as a proportion of total private flows because of the recent substantial increases in the flow of portfolio investment, especially in the form of bank lending to the developing countries. At the end of 1977, just under half the stock of private foreign investment in developing countries was of U.S. origin.

In terms of regional distribution by host area, Latin America was the major recipient, with 47 percent of the stock. In terms of sectoral distribution, investment in petroleum remained at 33.3 percent between 1965 and 1972. The stock of investment in manufacturing was also about one-

[3] United Nations, *Transnational Corporations in World Development: A Reexamination* (New York: United Nations, 1978), pp. 251 and 71.

third of the total in 1972, but the trend in its share was rising.

Affiliates of U.S.-based companies are generally wholly owned, although the trend is toward an increasing share of minority-owned firms. In Europe and especially in Japan, the trend is predominantly toward minority-owned subsidiaries.

Resources flow to affiliates of multinationals not only as capital but also in the form of technology and management. However, these flows are relatively difficult to measure and compare.

THREE

An Overview of the Problem

Any generalization about relationships between developing countries and multinational corporations inevitably oversimplifies a highly complex problem. Developing countries represent a wide diversity of colonial experiences, market sizes, political orientations, stages of development, and cultural attributes. Similarly, multinational corporations cover a broad spectrum in terms of the strategic aspects of their operations; for example, basic differences exist in the ways in which firms relate to host countries, depending on whether they are primary-resource companies, manufacturing firms that produce mainly standardized products, or high-technology companies. As a consequence of the diversity on both sides, the attitude of each toward the other and the nature of the relationship can hardly be described in monolithic terms.

Nevertheless, it is fair to state that in much of the developing world, relations between transnational corporations and host countries have been marked by considerable tension. Among the causes have been certain inherent instabilities in the relationship, differences in assessments of the impact of foreign direct investment on development, and efforts by host countries-to maximize the net social benefits accruing from the local operations of multinational firms.

STRAIN AND INSTABILITY

Much of the early strain in the relationship between host countries and multinational firms following World War II reflected an understandable determination on the part of many developing nations to consolidate political and economic control after long periods of foreign domination.

This effort, which involved extensive government intervention, was often viewed by multinationals as ideologically antithetical to a free enterprise system and therefore to their operations.

By the late 1960s, however, it became increasingly clear to the firms that the heart of the problem had little to do with ideology. In fact, some of the most stable and mutually profitable arrangements, including joint ventures and technology-sale agreements, have been negotiated between multinational companies and the socialist countries of Eastern Europe. With their strong governments and a clear sense of national purpose, these countries have, by and large, been able to offer the transnational companies firm and well-defined conditions without fear of being taken over or dominated.

With few exceptions, multinational companies today point to instability, not ideology, as the principal deterrent to investing and operating abroad. By instability, the companies do not necessarily mean political upheavals accompanied by changes in regime. Foreign investment does, of course, fall off during such a crisis but tends to recover as the new regime consolidates its position. Much more important are those forms of instability that need not result from internal political upheavals: threats of political action, changes in conditions of operation such as ownership and remittance regulations, complex and drawn-out bureaucratic procedures, and more generally, the prospect of arbitrary and unpredictable alterations in the rules of the game after investment decisions have been made. Although companies have come to expect and live with changes in government policy and regulation both at home and abroad and to recognize that such changes often reflect legitimate responses to altered conditions, they nevertheless perceive the degree of instability and arbitrariness of government policies in many developing countries as especially acute.

If instability is a key deterrent to investment, why is it that countries seeking to attract foreign enterprise do not adopt a more stable regulatory environment within which firms can operate? Indeed, some have tried to do so. In most cases, however, the inherent forces making for instability have been overwhelming in countries attempting to grapple with massive poverty, explosive population growth, and other problems endemic to the Third World. As these countries undergo the social and economic transformation that constitutes development, it is likely that multinational corporations will continue to face unpredictable changes in policies and rules related to foreign investment.

It is possible to draw up a long catalog of specific tension-creating problems in the relations between developing countries and multinationals, and in fact, the most important of these issues are raised in the interviews conducted for this project. However, it is possible to identify five forces of a more general and fundamental nature that inescapably lead to instability and tension in the foreign direct investment relationship.

Rapid Growth and Increased Bargaining Power

Rapid growth gives increased bargaining power to developing countries. A high rate of increase in both overall GNP and GNP per capita, such as that experienced over the last decade and a half in Brazil, Mexico, Taiwan, Korea, Thailand, Malaysia, and other countries, is attractive to foreign capital from several points of view. It means a rapidly growing domestic economy as measured by the increase in total GNP; it may also mean that the threshold has been crossed for an even more quickly expanding internal market for the type of discretionary products in which many multinationals specialize. At the same time, a sustained record of rapid increase in GNP *per capita* may signify the existence of those qualities of labor, infrastructure, and institutions that attract foreign enterprise to invest in production not only for the local market but also for export.

As developing countries experience rapid economic growth, they gradually become aware of their increased power in bargaining with multinationals. Indigenous firms may master the existing standard technology and thereby undermine the basis for the incentives and priorities accorded to the foreign firms. Transnationals based in different home countries may compete for rights to establish operations in a particular country. Other options materialize for acquiring finance and technology through the international banking and consulting networks. As these developments occur, the conditions of regulation and control applying to foreign enterprise inevitably change.

Altered National Goals

As countries undergo profound economic and social change, their national goals may be altered. For example, at some stage in its development, a country may place a high priority on industrialization. Industrialization is often pursued initially on the basis of import-substitution policies that are carried out through a wide range of regulations and in-

centives, such as the subsidization of domestic production of manufactured goods through high levels of protection against imports of finished
products, low protection on imports of intermediate and capital goods
not yet produced at home, and domestic-content requirements to increase the proportion of domestic value added. As the home market becomes saturated with domestic goods and the limits of import substitution become apparent, a country may shift to a policy of export
promotion involving a devaluation of its overvalued currency, a drastic
overhaul of the system of protection, and the adoption of a wide variety
of inducements and penalties to encourage exports. However, as export-
oriented growth proceeds, new priorities may emerge stressing other
economic and social goals such as job creation and income redistribution. Such shifting priorities are inevitable, and they frequently
produce uncertainty about the conditions under which private enterprise is permitted to operate.

The Obsolescing Bargain

The obsolescing bargain comes into play with particular force in the
case of investments in natural resources. Such ventures often entail high
risks at the outset and huge initial expenditures, but host countries frequently lack the resources necessary to develop their raw materials. In
order to attract firms to sink their capital under conditions of great uncertainty, host governments have typically granted long-term concessions
affording the companies a good deal of discretion in the conduct of their
operations and high returns if the ventures pan out. However, once the
investments are in place and the mines and other facilities are working
successfully, both parties may experience altered perceptions of what
constitutes a fair deal and may request renegotiation. Inevitably,
changes are forced in the terms of the arrangements having to do with
such vital elements as the volume of production, control of the operations, pricing of the product, and the division of the profits.

Scapegoating

Transnational enterprises can serve as convenient scapegoats in both
industrial and developing countries when governments are unable to sat-
isfy the needs and aspirations of their people. Because transnationals are
big, they draw the hostility of those who see them as smothering the
small local entrepreneur and threatening to dominate the domestic
economy. Because transnationals are foreign, they are seen as alien

influences subverting the indigenous culture and acting as tools of their home states. Because they are private, they are viewed as rapacious pursuers of their own gain at the expense of the public welfare. These stereotypes, deeply imbedded in popular thinking, can be effectively used to deflect and channel mass discontent regardless of the objective performance of multinationals at home and abroad.

Succession of Dilemmas

Third World governments face a series of frustrating dilemmas as they seek to shape a national policy toward foreign direct investment. If multinationals repatriate the bulk of their profits, they are depriving the nation of the newly created wealth; if, on the other hand, the firms reinvest the bulk of their profits locally, they are further increasing their ownership and control of the economy of the host country. If multinationals pay local workers the standard wage, they are exploiting cheap labor and garnering excess profits; if, on the other hand, they pay more than the prevailing wage, they are siphoning off the best of the labor supply and rendering local firms noncompetitive. If multinationals bring in the latest and best machinery and equipment, they are introducing inappropriate technology and diminishing job opportunities in the host country; if, on the other hand, earlier and simpler technologies are introduced, they are shortchanging the local economy. Resolving these dilemmas has entailed policy shifts and adaptations on the part of developing countries in response to their changing perceptions of how to maximize their gains from the foreign investment process.[1]

EVALUATING THE CONTRIBUTION OF
MULTINATIONALS TO DEVELOPMENT

Foreign investment is occasionally denounced on the grounds that it takes out of poor countries more than it puts in. This type of argument, particularly common among Latin American critics in the 1950s and 1960s, is based on a comparison of two annual financial flows: outflow of profits from the developing countries to the multinationals and net inflows of capital from the multinationals to the host countries. Indeed, an excess of outflows of profits over inflows of capital has existed for

[1] Raymond Vernon, *Storm Over the Multinationals: The Real Issues* (Cambridge, Mass.: Harvard University Press, 1977), Chapter 7, especially pp. 159-160.

many years. In 1974, the latest year for which global data are available, the multinationals repatriated profits of more than $16 billion from developing nations but brought in only $7 billion in new capital.

However, a simple comparison of these two flows does not make sense. To begin with, the flows are logically unrelated; the outflow of profits in a given year is related to investments in prior years, not to the inflow of capital in the same year. Futhermore, as a statement of the balance-of-payments effects of foreign direct investment, it is grossly misleading to look at only one item of receipts (capital inflows) and compare it with one item of payments (profit remittances). It is necessary to look instead at the impact of foreign investment on all items in a country's balance of payments, including the effect on the volume of imports and exports. In the case of natural resource investment, for example, the bulk of the output is typically exported from the host country, contributing to net foreign exchange receipts on the trade account; whereas in manufacturing, the output may be sold in the domestic market in partial substitution for imports.

The more fundamental question relates, not to the balance-of-payments consequences of foreign investment, but to the effect on the host country's real income. The essence of the case for foreign investment (and presumably the reason most Third World countries try to encourage it) is that it brings in a package of resources that adds to the output (value added) and real income of the host country an amount greater than that appropriated by the investor. The increase in income that is not appropriated by the investor must accrue to other groups; it may benefit labor in the form of higher real wages, consumers in the form of lower prices, and the government in the form of higher tax revenues.

As a first approximation, therefore, it ought to be possible to calculate the total benefit of foreign investment to the host economy and to divide that total among the beneficiaries. Actually, labor's gain may consist not only of higher wages made possible by greater productivity but also of more employment. This may be particularly important where population and labor force growth rates are high, as they are in many developing countries. The gains to consumers may consist not only of lower prices but also of a wider choice of better-quality products. As for government revenues, taxes on the profits of foreign enterprises constitute a large portion of the total tax receipts of many developing countries. In fact, tax collections as a proportion of GNP are often highest in developing countries that have received substantial foreign investment.

If profitable foreign investment benefits not only the investor but also these various local beneficiaries, why has so much controversy surrounded the impact of transnationals on economic development? Setting aside the question of the internal distribution of the gains within the host country, is it not obvious that so long as the investment meets the market test of profitability, it cannot be a zero-sum game but must be one of mutual benefit to both foreign enterprise and host country? This question can be answered in terms of four sets of considerations: externalities, distortions, attribution, and alternatives.

Externalities

Some of the most important effects of foreign investment are external to the firm in the sense that they are not reflected in calculations based on market-determined costs of inputs and prices of outputs. In recent years, we have learned a good deal about externalities in connection with environmental pollution. A firm that pollutes the atmosphere imposes a social cost on the community that is not captured in the company's private accounting but that must be considered in estimating its net social product. Similarly, multinationals impose social costs on, and yield social benefits to, host countries that are not reflected in the firms' private accounting.

The external benefits are of many different kinds: Foreign enterprise may stimulate domestic entrepreneurship directly by purchasing from, or subcontracting to, local suppliers and indirectly through demonstration effects such as proving the existence of a local market for a new product. It may also provide a boost to host-country industries that produce goods bought by the workers who have higher real wages as a result of the presence of the foreign firm. If the foreign enterprise invests in a bottleneck sector, it may induce expansion of production in other sectors with underutilized capacity that are dependent on inputs from the bottleneck sector. The investment may thereby make possible hitherto unrealized economies of scale. If foreign enterprise trains workers in new skills, their knowledge may spread to other members of the labor force, or the newly trained workers may be hired later by local companies. Technology introduced by foreign firms may find uses elsewhere in the economy, leading to lower costs and improved products. And the entry of a foreign firm may result in a more efficient local market structure by bringing competitive pressure to bear on the comfortable position enjoyed by a local monopolist.

Any assessment of these social benefits, however, must be tempered by a realization that there may also be social costs. A foreign enterprise, drawing on the vast technical and managerial resources of its parent company, may snuff out newly emerging local entrepreneurs. By borrowing locally, it may also deprive indigenous firms of their main source of capital. The new technology introduced by the multinationals may be highly capital-intensive and thus fail to utilize labor fully even where unemployment is already widespread. Far from encouraging competition, the foreign enterprise may itself become a monopolist in the local market. By locating production in the most advanced regions of the host country, the firm may increase inequalities among income groups and regions. Moreover, its product may cater to the sophisticated, high-income consumption pattern of those who are relatively well-off while stimulating unrealistic wants on the part of the bulk of the population.

To list even illustratively these external benefits and costs may be sufficient to convey a sense of the difficulties involved in a quantitative assessment of the contribution of foreign investment on a general level. Perhaps useful results can be obtained from social cost-benefit analysis for some individual projects.[2] As our interviews suggest, however, the opinions of multinationals on the social consequences of their operations often diverge widely from the views of host-country critics. The most helpful practical contribution to the debate may therefore be to seek ideas about how to reduce the social costs and increase the social benefits, whatever their precise magnitude, rather than to attempt to quantify the net social contribution of the present operations of transnational firms to development.

Distortions

Difficulties of evaluation may also arise because the private accounting of a firm may itself be distorted by actions taken by the host government or the transnational. If the firm produces goods for the host-country market, its output as measured by value added may be exaggerated by

[2] For quantitative attempts to assess the impact of foreign investment on national income and the balance of payments, see the OECD-sponsored study by H. C. Bos, Martin Sanders, and Carlo Secchi, *Private Foreign Investment in Developing Countries* (Boston: D. Reidel Publishing Company, 1974), and the UNCTAD-sponsored study by Sanjaya Lall and Paul Streeten, *Foreign Investment, Transnationals, and Developing Countries* (London: Macmillan Press, 1977). These studies, based on samples of a limited number of developing countries (five for Bos, Sanders, and Secchi and six for Lall and Streeten), yield inconclusive results.

artificially high prices for its products that are a result of tariffs or other
government restrictions on imports of comparable products. At the same
time, imported equipment, components, and materials may be obtained
at artificially low prices because of an overvalued exchange rate maintained by the government through a system of exchange controls. Similarly, direct government subsidies, tax holidays, and other forms of incentives may result in costs of inputs and prices of outputs that deviate
from their true social accounting prices, which are based on relative
scarcity.

Distortions may also occur because of the situation or policies of the
firm itself. The multinational may possess some unique advantage—
such as a special technology, a trademark, or simply a local market too
small to warrant the entry of another firm—that permits it to charge a
higher price for its products than it could in a more competitive market.
Or the firm may set arbitrary transfer prices on its intracorporate transactions. For tax or other reasons, it may shift taxable income from the host
country to other jurisdictions. In that case, the company might pay
artificially high prices for supplies from its parent and affiliates and sell
products to them at artificially low prices.

In evaluating the contribution of foreign investment to development,
corrections need to be made for these types of distortions. The process is
similar in principle to that for taking account of externalities. Both involve assigning "shadow prices" that correspond more closely to the
real costs of inputs to society and the real benefits of outputs in place of
actual prices. Although shadow pricing is a most imprecise art, it is perhaps less subject to serious error when it is applied to distortions than
when it is applied to externalities because of the greater likelihood of the
existence of price data reflecting the realities of economic scarcity.

Attribution

At the base of much of the controversy surrounding the evaluation of
the role of multinationals in developing countries is the confusion arising
from mistaken attribution. For example, if a country's overvalued exchange rate encourages a firm to import more machinery and employ
less labor than it otherwise would, is the firm to be blamed, or is the
problem one of government policy? If a foreign enterprise locates a new
plant in the capital of a country because of ample supplies of skilled labor, transportation, and other infrastructure, is its neglect of the more
critical social need for new investment in the country's more backward

regions related to the foreignness or transnationality of the firm, or is it a reflection of the normal decision-making process in any private firm, domestic or foreign? Does the remedy lie in some special government action directed at foreign firms or in more general government incentives or disincentives designed to adjust private investment decision making in line with the host country's broader social objectives?

Alternatives

Logically, any assessment of the net effects of foreign investment should specify the situation with which it is being compared. In the case of a foreign investment to produce for the local market, the host country presumably has a number of alternatives: It can import the product; a local firm might raise the capital and other resources domestically and set up a plant; the capital might be borrowed abroad and the technology and management hired through a licensing agreement; or a joint venture might be set up involving the mobilization of both domestic and foreign resources.

With the exception of importing, however, these theoretical alternatives may not always be available. For example, although capital might be borrowed independently, know-how might not be obtainable in a particular case except through direct investment by a foreign firm. Therefore, a precise and detailed consideration of available alternatives cannot take place at the macroeconomic level; such an evaluation is possible only at the level of individual projects.

In sum, it is apparent that major difficulties and uncertainties surround any effort to evaluate the impact of foreign investment on developing countries. Among the principal problems are estimating the external social and economic effects, identifying and correcting for distortions in the pricing of inputs and outputs, properly attributing the blame for the costs and the credit for the benefits associated with foreign investment, and specifying and taking due account of the alternatives against which a foreign investment is to be compared.

MAXIMIZING THE GAINS

Although political rhetoric about dependency and exploitation continues in some forums, both transnational corporations and developing countries are increasingly aware that the impact of foreign enterprise on development is not a subject for broad generalization. They have come to realize that transnationals can have a spectrum of effects and that the task of policy is to maximize beneficial effects and to minimize detrimental effects.

Transnational enterprises cannot be forced to do business in a particular country; they can only be attracted. Most developing countries have designed special programs of incentives and concessions to attract multinational firms, sometimes at substantial cost to the local economy. But by far the most important factors in attracting foreign firms are the relative stability of the general political, social, and economic conditions and the prospect of earning a profit without relying on special government favors. Transnationals will accept or even welcome special inducements, but unless the fundamental conditions for doing business are right, they will be reluctant to enter a country under circumstances that require a substantial commitment of their own financial or other resources.

Similarly, developing countries cannot be forced to accept foreign direct investment; they must see that the net benefits of a proposed project are greater than those of available alternatives. Third World governments, dedicated to improving the economic and social conditions under which their people live, face tasks of enormous difficulty. It is understandable that they are determined to use all available resources to overcome those problems.

Therefore, host countries seek not only to attract foreign investment but also to harness it to their goals. Sometimes these goals may conflict, requiring trade-offs among, for example, the economic objective of maximizing output and tax revenues, the social objective of equalizing income distribution, and the political objective of increasing domestic managerial control over foreign enterprise. There are no simple rules that will apply to all cases.

The tools for attempting to maximize the contribution of multinationals to host-country goals are direct regulation and the use of market incentives and disincentives. How these tools are deployed depends on the nature of the foreign investment and the relative bargaining power of the parties. The bargaining relationship is likely to differ for the three basic models of foreign investment: natural resource projects, manufacturing investments to serve the local market, and manufacturing investments primarily for export. Typically (but by no means always), host-country leverage will be greater in the first two instances than it will be in the third, in which acceptable alternative countries from which to export are likely to be available. Moreover, the bargaining position of the host country will tend to strengthen over time in the case of natural resource ventures because of substantial front-end commitments on the part of the transnational enterprise. On the other hand, high-technology manufacturing firms serving the local market are likely to retain their bargaining power longer than firms using standardized technology because the contribution of high-technology companies depends on a continuing inflow of resources from the parent in the form of new technology.

Bargaining relationships also vary with the stage of development and the degree of sophistication of the host country. The stereotype of weak and technically uninformed nations as no match for the negotiating skills of powerful transnationals is undoubtedly true in some cases but certainly not in others. For example, Brazil, the most important Third World host to foreign investment, believes it has the power and skill to influence the behavior of the transnationals:

> We must accept the reality of the existence of multinational enter-
> prises. To deny this would be to shun reality. Yet we believe that it is per-
> fectly possible to neutralize the evils that multinationals can cause and
> take advantage of the benefits that they can bring to our economy. . . .
> We have all the means to exercise control over the multinationals.[3]

Smaller and weaker countries, on the other hand, require various forms of assistance—legal, technical, and financial—in negotiating with multinational firms and in regulating their activities.

The bargaining process is a subtle art. Over time, the total investment gains to be divided between host country and multinational are unlikely to be independent of how the shares are divided. A cooperative approach may expand the total gains and increase the absolute returns to both sides. Such an outcome can be facilitated by a better mutual understanding of the attitudes and perceptions of each side. Parts II and III, which analyze the attitudes of transnational corporations toward problems identified by host countries, are intended as a contribution toward a more satisfactory solution.

[3] Statement made by Shigaeki Ueki, Brazilian minister of mines and energy, in 1976 as quoted in Stefan H. Robock, "Controlling Multinational Enterprises: The Brazilian Experience," *Journal of Contemporary Business* (Autumn 1977): 62.

Part II

The Interview Results

FOUR

The Interview Results:
An Introduction

Part II presents the results of the interviews for each subject or closely related group of subjects. In each case, we begin with a succinct statement of the issues. Wherever appropriate, the issue statements are presented from the perspective of the developing countries. These views have been derived mainly from the voluminous literature on the role of transnational corporations in developing countries, much of it published in the form of U.N. studies and reports.[1]

After outlining the issue, we summarize the responses of the transnational firms, identifying, where possible, the convergence and divergence of their evolving views. The interview results clearly show that among both companies and countries, a wide diversity of opinions and policies exists, reflecting variations in size, economic specialization, and historical experience. These differences naturally affect the relationship be-

---

[1] In addition to the volumes by individual authors cited in Part I, several basic U.N. documents provide an excellent overview of Third World concerns. These publications include *Multinational Corporations in World Development* (1973); *The Impact of Multinational Corporations on the Development Process and on International Relations: Report of the Group of Eminent Persons to Study the Role of Multinational Corporations on Development and on International Relations* (1974); *Transnational Corporations: Issues Involved in the Formulation of a Code of Conduct* (1976); *Transnational Corporations: Material Relevant to the Formulation of a Code of Conduct* (1977); and *Transnational Corporations in World Development: A Reexamination* (1978). All the foregoing studies were published by the United Nations in New York.

tween the two groups, the importance of particular problems for individual countries and companies, and their attitudes on specific issues.

As summarized in Parts II and III of the study, the views of the respondents are presented, not as facts, but as the attitudes of executives experienced in corporate activities in the Third World. They do not necessarily reflect the opinions of the author or the sponsoring organizations, nor has any attempt been made to evaluate the responses.

Although the interviews were conducted in a frank and open atmosphere, we cannot claim total accuracy or candor in the answers. Throughout the study, where views are ascribed to companies, they reflect the opinions of the executives who were interviewed and may not be the official views of the companies.

FIVE

Dichotomy of National and Corporate Goals

The Issues

Developing countries commonly perceive affiliates of foreign firms as single-mindedly pursuing goals determined by their parent companies. Those corporate goals may relate to such matters as profit maximization, diversifying raw material supplies, preempting or maintaining a foreign market position, and achieving some rate of overall growth in sales or earnings.

The national goals are of a different order. They may include such broad social and economic objectives as maximizing tax revenues and employment, stimulating exports, developing local technological and entrepreneurial capacity, encouraging smaller industries and development in rural areas, improving income distribution, and developing neglected regions.

Among the issues raised by these differences are whether the national goals are clearly articulated and understood, whether the dichotomy between the two sets of aims necessarily implies conflict, and what the relative responsibilities of multinational corporation and host country are in bringing company operations into conformity with national objectives.

Related issues are whether local participation in ownership and management of foreign affiliates is an effective way of reconciling the divergence between company and national goals and the extent to which such

conflict as exists reflects the difference between private and public objectives regardless of a firm's nationality.

The Responses

How clearly developing countries express their national goals and
how well multinationals understand them depend on the particular country and company in question. The majority of multinational corporations
gave Asian countries, particularly Malaysia and India, high marks for
the clarity with which they express their general development objectives. African nations, with the exception of Nigeria, were also seen as
having well-defined goals. The transnationals evaluated Latin American
and Caribbean countries less favorably in this respect. Brazil was the
South American country most frequently cited as having clear, well-
articulated aims, and Colombia was also mentioned. But opinions dif-
fered about how articulate Peru and Mexico are in stating their goals,
and Jamaica was not perceived as having clear objectives.

Transnationals pointed out that, as in more developed countries, there
is likely to be a certain amount of inconsistency, internal disagreement,
and fluidity in Third World national goals. An example of such inconsistency is the conflicting goals of maximizing both employment and exports. A host country may require that corporations build small-scale,
labor-intensive facilities and may then tell them to export despite the
high costs of this method of production for some products. Another type
of inconsistency may be between goals and their feasibility. However
clear the aims, policy measures for achieving them may be economically
unrealistic. Respondents also noted that conflicts can arise between the
goals of neighboring countries; for example, both may want the same
company to export into each other's market.

Most transnationals felt that Third World countries generally do a
good job of articulating their goals despite these inconsistencies but recognized the inevitable dichotomy between national and corporate goals.
Furthermore, several companies said that a distinction must be made between the public rhetoric of developing nations regarding the aims and
effects of transnationals and their attitudes and performance in private
negotiations. While lambasting the corporations in international forums, host-country officials often prove in pragmatic negotiations that
they appreciate the benefits the multinationals can bring to the local
economy.

Although the firms did not say so explicitly, there was an implication that conflicts may be due more to inherent differences between private and public objectives than to tensions between corporate and local goals. For example, several Swedish, British, American, and Australian companies asserted that it is often local enterprise, rather than the multinational, that shows the greatest disregard for host-country aims. Multinationals argued that for a number of reasons they are in a more vulnerable position than domestic industry and therefore have to be more in tune with such goals. The response of one British manufacturer reflected the sentiments of several corporate officials; he characterized some local entrepreneurs as "rapacious, greedy, utterly ruthless, and often incapable of understanding why anyone should bother about national goals." As an illustration of this point, a Swedish firm cited a local competitor in Latin America who dismissed personnel prior to retirement in order to avoid pension payments. The Swedish company observed that a foreign-owned firm could not safely take such action even if it were so inclined.

Despite the majority viewpoint that some conflict is inevitable, several foreign enterprises, particularly those producing consumer goods, indicated that they make a more conscious effort to bring their operations into line with national goals because they are aware of their limited bargaining power in disputes with the host-country government.

Few companies argued that the conflicts are fundamental or irreconcilable. Respondents noted that the disagreements are usually on matters of detail and degree and are less important than the underlying community of interest. In some countries, however, the conditions laid down by host governments (e.g., India) have been unacceptable to some companies, which have therefore either refrained from investing or ceased operations. In Malaysia, the hiring of particular ethnic groups is subject to restrictions that, in the view of an American firm, can critically affect its decision to remain in the country.

Because the transnationals saw the majority of clashes over goals as reconcilable, they generally suggested that differences be resolved through negotiation and compromise. They felt that in most disputes the company should go along with the host country as far as it reasonably can. This may involve some short-term disadvantages, but over the long run, the company stands to gain from showing that it is a "good corporate citizen."

One European company has found that there are three types of government with which it negotiates: One is sympathetic to private enterprise and understands its needs. In such cases, few conflicts arise, and those that do are easily reconciled. A second type simply does not understand the requirements of private industry. In negotiations with such governments, many difficulties surface and take a great deal of time to resolve. The third type of government is openly hostile to private industry. In this case, conflicts are even sharper, although some accommodation may be worked out.

A minority of British and American firms said that they would not invest unless the developing country did the bulk of the adjusting. According to this view, the multinational must communicate its needs to the potential host country, which must then try to meet them. These firms argued that their ability to make a profit should not be hindered by a country's pursuit of its national goals.

One possible way in which companies could increase Third World awareness of the benefits of their operations would be for the firms to demonstrate through specific accounting or information systems how they are serving the national priorities of host countries. With few exceptions, transnationals have no such systems (although several said they try to convey the same points in their annual reports). In many cases, this information would be made available to the host government on request. Certain Japanese firms suggested that methods be developed to measure the multinational's social contributions to developing countries. These methods could be similar to the public-disclosure criteria for corporate accounting being deliberated by the United Nations Commission on Transnational Corporations.

Most transnationals stated that they would like to see host countries express national objectives clearly in a framework of laws and regulations that the companies could then take into account before deciding whether to invest. The general feeling was that if national goals are stated in this fashion, the firms can accommodate to them. Firms also felt that developing countries should tone down antimultinational rhetoric ("the generals are fighting the last war") and employ civil servants who have practical experience in dealing with foreign-owned enterprise.

SIX

Fields of Investment

EFFECTS ON LOCAL COMPETITION
AND ENTREPRENEURSHIP

The Issues

There are two related aspects to this issue: One concerns the effect of the entry of a foreign firm on existing or potential local firms in the same business; the other concerns the effect of the marketing practices of foreign firms in shaping or "distorting" local tastes and creating a form of cultural dependency.

The first aspect lays stress on how local entrepreneurs are smothered when multinationals, with their tremendous technological and financial resources, establish subsidiaries in developing countries. Existing firms may be forced out of business or may decide to sell out to the multinationals. Moreover, barriers are created to the entry of new, indigenous entrepreneurs as a consequence of the advertising, promotion, and product-differentiation practices of multinationals.

At the same time, the latter practices lead to the second dimension of the Third World's concern: the stimulation by multinationals of a demand for types of products too sophisticated for, or otherwise inappropriate to, a poor country's stage of development. Critics frequently point to the promotion of formula foods for infants as a substitute for breast-feeding and highly advertised soft drinks based on imported ingredients or technology. The marketing practices of the multinationals are therefore seen as suppressing local entrepreneurs not only by direct competition but also by capitalizing on and reinforcing a strong prejudice in favor of foreign products, brand names, and trademarks. This is regarded as objectionable not only in economic terms but also because it perpetuates a form of sociocultural dependence rooted in the colonial experience from which the developing countries seek emancipation.

The Responses

The views of multinational corporations on their effects on local competition and entrepreneurship vary largely by the industry sector of their subsidiaries rather than by the nationality of the parent company. Not surprisingly, the higher the level of technology, the less overlap there is between the subsidiary's product and that of locally owned enterprise.

Firms that are in the business of extracting natural resources have generally found that they face little or no local competition. Because of the high capital requirements and complex technologies required by the extractive industries, it is difficult for private indigenous entrepreneurs to enter the field. What competition there is usually comes from other foreign-owned subsidiaries or state-owned enterprises, although in such areas as marketing, refining, and other processing activities, competition occasionally comes from local entrepreneurs as well. Where local competition does exist, extractive companies reported that it is frequently protected by regulations that may give it certain advantages. For example, the host government may reserve prime sites for nationals.

In manufacturing, there is a clear distinction between high-technology industries and other types of firms.[1] High-technology companies indicated that their competition is overwhelmingly limited to subsidiaries of other transnationals. Only in three instances did high-technology firms (all based in the United States) report that they have effective indigenous competition. In two of these cases, subsidiaries face competition in India and Brazil, where the markets are sufficiently large to support several firms and where host-government regulation provides special incentives to local industries.

With the exception of some British and Japanese companies, manufacturing firms outside the high-technology sector stated that local competition not only exists but also may be quite active. In many cases, however, the subsidiaries' products are of superior quality because of more stringent production and packaging standards, and several of the firms

[1] *High-technology* manufacturing firms are those companies that depend on a continuous flow of technology.

felt that this gives them a competitive edge. The major exception in this group is the automotive corporations. They reported that their competition is primarily foreign-owned.

Most of the British and Japanese said they do not experience effective competition from locally owned firms, although competition from other subsidiaries is sometimes present. This lack of indigenous competition was attributed to conscious corporate policy. The British tend to invest only in sizable markets that are not already being served by efficient local producers. One firm has actually moved out of areas of production as indigenous enterprises have become able to compete. The Japanese companies do not produce goods that would compete with locally made products in the local market; instead, they manufacture for the Japanese and other markets.

Multinationals in the service industries compete to some extent with local enterprises, but in many cases, banking and retail firms are complementary. The banking industry, for example, is highly regulated; and in many developing countries, foreign banks are limited in the kinds of services they are allowed to provide. Thus, although both foreign and local banks may exist in the same country, they are frequently not in direct competition with each other. U.S. banks observed that they seldom hold a dominant or even a conspicuous position in a developing country's banking industry. This was less true of banks based in home countries with a colonial background. The strong, early presence of these banks in what are now independent countries may have made it more difficult for local banks to get started.

Retailers recognized that they may force marginal local merchants out of business, but they noted that direct competition with local merchants is usually minimal because foreign retailers tend to appeal to higher-income consumers and to expand that segment of the market. Foreign retailers also said they try to concentrate on kinds of business operations that are more difficult to organize, such as large department stores. Although mass buyers are attracted to the large retail stores, neighboring merchants get the spillover from the extremes of the consumer scale, which expands the market and better serves consumers' needs.

Many firms, particularly in the high-technology sector, recognized that their presence in developing countries frequently tends to prevent local firms from entering a particular product line. However, they generally believed that this is because of their technology, know-how, and capital, which are beyond the capabilities of local entrepreneurs, rather than because of their promotional, advertising, and other marketing advantages. With few exceptions, none of the firms felt that smothering (forcing an existing enterprise out of business) is a serious problem. Indeed, one European firm found that in countries experiencing high rates of growth, some local entrepreneurs have been tempted to abandon their industrial operations, not because of competition from transnationals, but in order to speculate in such areas as real estate.

Where smothering does occur, the multinationals argued that it results from the inefficiency of indigenous industry, not from the overwhelming presence of a transnational. Two non-U.S.-based firms suggested that any problems caused by the displacement of inefficient firms would be largely social, psychological, and political because the presence of efficient foreign enterprises is advantageous to a host country in economic terms. Several high-technology corporations mentioned instances in which a subsidiary, rather than a local firm, failed in the face of competition. Other firms conceded that the entry of new enterprises might be discouraged in countries where a multinational has an established position. Even in such cases, however, local companies often find it possible to operate. They may, for example, use simpler packaging or lower-quality ingredients to create a product that appeals to a different type of consumer.

The companies felt that there are many reasons why charges of smothering are not valid. The extractive and high-technology manufacturing firms in particular pointed out that the lack of indigenous industry means that there is no overlapping of products. Several companies stated that local enterprises may have specific advantages such as lower overhead costs, government support, and priority access to local financial resources that help to keep them competitive with the subsidiaries of transnationals. However, German-based corporations generally felt that such advantages are of minimal value and do not substantially diminish the superior position of the foreign firm.

Extractive and manufacturing companies asserted that their operations actually promote local entrepreneurship, both in their own fields and in ancillary activities, through such means as local-content requirements,[2] joint ventures, forward linkages, and training of local employees who may go on to start their own businesses. In the petroleum industry, for example, the multinational frequently provides the com-

---

[2] *Local-content requirements* are requirements mandated by a government for the use of locally produced materials and components in further processing and manufacturing.

plex storage and distribution facilities, but locally owned service stations handle the retailing. The establishment of mining towns encourages many domestic businesses to provide a variety of goods and services to people living in the towns.

The issue of distorted patterns of consumption as a result of the introduction of inappropriate products was less clearly addressed by the multinationals. The issue has limited applicability in the case of extractive firms unless the subsidiaries are also involved in processing and manufacturing. However, it does arise in the retailing segment of the service industries. A retailer observed that although his company's stock of goods must be based on the tastes and preferences of local consumers, it is also the firm's responsibility to make available goods that will improve the life-style, productivity, and comfort of a host country's population. For this reason, the firm continually "brings to their attention" various products that are outside traditional local consumption patterns.

Manufacturers producing consumer goods seem to be quite responsive to consumer needs and tastes. Local variations tend to be greatest in products where there are wide differences in personal taste, as in the case of food and textiles, or where differences in climatic conditions must be taken into account, as in the case of vehicle components and clothing. In contrast, firms engaged in high-technology manufacturing usually produce intermediate or capital goods. These companies frequently stressed the importance of worldwide product uniformity both in maintaining quality and in providing a servicing network with interchangeable parts and components. A number of manufacturing firms stated that their presence in developing countries tends to "upgrade" the quality of competing products produced locally, a phenomenon that is assumed to be inherently good.

For the most part, the manufacturers interviewed contended that they are trying to meet the existing tastes of local consumers rather than to create new ones. Moreover, two high-technology manufacturing firms (one American, the other Swedish) felt that the issue of distorted consumption patterns is largely rhetoric. Both cited examples of attempts to use technologically less sophisticated goods more suited to the needs of the particular countries that were firmly rejected by the host governments, which insisted on the most advanced products. Other firms, without citing specific examples, also referred to the Catch-22 of either "distorting" consumption patterns or dumping junk products and obsolete technologies.

EFFECTS OF PROTECTION OF HOST-COUNTRY
MARKETS AGAINST COMPETING IMPORTS

The Issues

Many developing countries, especially those that have relatively large populations and gross national products, have sought to conserve foreign exchange and encourage industrialization by providing a high degree of protection to domestic manufacturing. The criticism is that multinational firms are often in the best position to take advantage of this implicit subsidy by locating their subsidiaries behind the protective barriers. As a consequence, the stimulus to industrialization often fails to benefit indigenous enterprise, and the local economy bears the cost in terms of higher prices and possibly of excessive profits for the foreign firms.

More specifically, the transnational corporation is sometimes seen as encouraging excessive protection or discouraging the phasing out of import restrictions in order to preserve its captive market. Moreover, in the case of the company that engages primarily in assembly or packaging operations, the "effective" protection on local value added tends to exceed substantially the nominal rate of protection on the final product.[3]

Even when the protected foreign operations are regarded as contributing to the goals of conserving foreign exchange and encouraging indigenous manufacturing industries, developing countries believe that their governments should take positive steps to increase the benefits to the local economy. The governments should at least assure that multinationals insulated from foreign competition do not charge excessive prices or earn excessive profits.

However, some critics of multinationals do concede that many of the problems associated with import substitution[4] are not peculiar to foreign firms but apply more generally to protected manufacturing firms regardless of ownership.

[3] For example, suppose a company imports auto parts duty-free and assembles them locally into finished vehicles. Assume also that the imported parts constitute 90 percent of the value of the finished vehicle, and that the import duty on finished vehicles (as opposed to parts) is 20 percent. Although the nominal protection on the finished vehicle is only 20 percent, the effective protection on the 10 percent of the value of the auto produced locally is .20/.10, or 200 percent. In other words, the local assembler receives enough protection to enable him to incur costs in the assembly operation that exceed world market costs by 200 percent.

[4] *Import substitution* denotes the substitution of domestic production for imports as a result of policies to protect the home market.

The Responses

Multinationals in the manufacturing sector are affected the most by host-country policies that protect local markets. Companies engaged in extractive and service activities generally did not find the issue relevant to their experience.

Most manufacturing firms have found their investment decisions sharply influenced by host-country policies of sheltering home markets. Given the choice, multinationals would prefer to export from their home countries rather than produce locally. However, where host countries impose protective trade barriers, that option may not be available.

High-technology manufacturers in particular stated that import restrictions are a crucial motivating force in favor of the decision to move abroad. For example, some of the pharmaceutical firms said that it does not pay to manufacture in the host country. Economies of scale as well as the need for sophisticated skills and technology, including research and development and clinical experimentation, make "basic manufacture" of pharmaceuticals unfeasible in developing countries. Given minimal per-unit transportation costs, these pharmaceutical companies would almost always prefer to export from their home base to both developed and developing countries rather than manufacture locally. However, local packaging may make sense in the case of large markets. The pharmaceutical firms see the establishment of production subsidiaries in developing countries as the result of host-government intervention through import restrictions or other regulations, not of economic considerations. Similarly, firms that process natural resources locally and those in the automotive industry noted that restrictions have played a critical role in their decisions to invest in developing countries.

One U.S. firm said that import restrictions are imposed for balance-of-payments reasons rather than to protect local industry. The only reason this company produces in developing countries is to earn foreign exchange with which to import its own products. That is, the subsidiary manufactures certain commodities in the host country for export and uses the foreign exchange earned in this fashion to import other goods the parent company produces.

Once firms become established locally, however, sheltered markets often become essential if subsidiaries are to survive and remain profitable. As one U.S. manufacturer observed, "The elimination of import restrictions could be disastrous to us in some places." Moreover, phasing out protection would affect domestic interests as well as foreign ones. One company that processes raw materials locally noted that the removal of protection would upset local business interests more than it would the parent firm because local private interests own a portion of the operation, and "they call the tune."

Market size and potential are even more important than protection in the decision to establish subsidiaries that will manufacture goods within the host-country market. A country must have attractive market opportunities before a transnational will invest in it. If the market potential exists, foreign manufacturing firms may establish local subsidiaries regardless of protection. Indeed, developing countries with sufficiently large markets can use the threat of protection as a means to induce foreign investment. For example, firms that manufacture "luxury" consumer goods prefer local production when a market appears to have potential. Such goods are not critical to a Third World country's economic development. Thus, the threat of import restrictions on nonessential consumer goods is always present and serves as a potent investment stimulus to corporations that want to sell these goods to developing countries.

Host-country policies designed to shelter the local market can, in fact, alter the balance between the benefits and costs of a potential investment in such a way that the gains to the firm outweigh the disadvantages. Clearly, no one factor can be said to be the sole determinant in the decision to invest in a developing country. Nevertheless, transnationals recognize that factors such as host-country import-substitution policies can be critical at the margin in affecting both the size and the location of foreign investment.

Although high-technology firms generally do not manufacture locally without protection, other companies are willing to set up local manufacturing facilities regardless of protection. Australian firms not operating in high-technology areas and companies producing bulk products such as paper goods or building materials said that high transportation costs make it too expensive to export from the home-country base. Such companies have found that local manufacturing is not only the most profitable means of servicing foreign markets but also results in lower costs to the host country.

Electronics and food-processing companies indicated that they set up production facilities overseas to take advantage of relatively cheap costs of labor and other factors of production. Several of these companies have been established in developing countries for many years, and they pointed out that at the time they went in, the countries did not have independent governments capable of pursuing protective policies.

The viewpoint of the multinationals has been that policies sheltering local markets have both positive and negative effects on the economic growth of the host countries, with the overall effect depending on how the policies are managed over time. Among the most frequently mentioned potential benefits were increased employment opportunities, upgrading of both technical and managerial skills, development of ancillary industries, better access to technology, and a general spur to industrialization. In addition, the companies cited higher tax revenues, foreign exchange savings, increased local value added through technological change and productivity improvements, and an increased rate of local capital formation resulting from reinvested earnings. However, a British firm stated that it is impossible to generalize about the benefits and costs to developing countries of restrictive import policies. Countries and companies differ; therefore, protection may be of benefit to some but not to others.

Most firms noted that protective policies also impose costs on developing countries, especially higher prices for locally produced goods. U.S. high-technology firms were the most vocal in asserting that protection leads to higher prices locally; such firms are characterized by significant economies of scale, tend to be capital-intensive, and face higher raw material costs in developing countries. One U.S. executive stated that a product his company manufactures in the United States "could be shipped to Uruguay for about $200, but it costs $600 to build one there."

In contrast, some Australian and Japanese companies argued that in the case of some industries, developing countries with sheltered local markets would ultimately benefit through goods that are higher in quality *and* lower in price. Temporary protection, they explained, provides manufacturers a period of shelter from outside competition during which economies external to the firm are realized. French enterprises also seemed generally to believe that the early additional costs of protection "will pay off later."

Many firms believed that developing countries can increase their share of the benefits while continuing to shelter their markets. A U.S. firm suggested that host countries apply benefit-cost analysis to alterna-

tive trade strategies and remove restrictions that hinder increases in productivity and employment. For example, importation of economical
secondhand equipment is sometimes prohibited by host governments
because they want the most technologically advanced equipment. One
U.S. manufacturer proposed that countries with large markets eliminate
restrictions "since levies on imported parts and components tend to en-
rich the customs authorities" while raising the costs of local production.
British and Australian firms felt that increasing the portion of locally
owned equity would increase the benefits of protective policies. However, one British firm argued that local participation should not exceed
50 percent. Other suggestions included increasing the proportion of local staff and establishing local-content requirements.

The multinationals cautioned developing countries not to move too
swiftly or too far in attempting to increase their share of the benefits because to do so might hinder their growth. For example, unrealistically
steep or rapid increases of local-content requirements could lower production efficiency and product quality.

Although both the transnationals and the host countries receive some
benefits as a result of protective policies, many manufacturers in the
United States, Japan, and Australia believed that both sides should re-
consider the net benefits and costs. Several firms were of the opinion that
protection should ultimately be phased out. The Japanese said that the
host-government provision of subsidies for an indefinite period of time
will tend to weaken the subsidized firms' competitiveness in the international market. An American executive complained that developing
countries are hurting themselves through their conflicting demands for
subsidiaries to produce locally and to export because subsidized firms
often cannot compete effectively in the world market. The higher per-
unit manufacturing costs incurred by such companies prohibit competitive exporting.

Finally, several American, British, French, and Swedish firms objected to the assertion that they reap a "subsidy"—that is, a benefit or
bonus—as a result of protective policies. They pointed out that so-called
subsidies in the form of higher prices for goods locally produced help to
offset the higher costs and increased risks of producing locally; therefore, the firms argued, they do not reap excessive profits. Indeed, one
American firm said that to the extent that a company is required by the
host government to buy higher-priced, protected local inputs, the company is, in effect, subject to a special tax.

ENTREPRENEURIAL FREEDOM

The Issues

Although a good deal of autonomy is accorded to local subsidiaries in day-to-day operations, representatives of Third World nations have claimed that parent companies give managers of local subsidiaries very little scope for exercising entrepreneurial initiative. For example, it is asserted that multinationals do not permit local managers (especially those who are not home-country nationals) to make decisions to diversify into related products beyond the parent firm's product line. Because they are kept on a tight tether, affiliates of foreign companies are seen as extensions of the parent firm rather than as integral parts of the local economy.

The Responses

The degree of entrepreneurial freedom given by parent firms to their subsidiaries appears to depend primarily on the product and technology involved and on the degree of parent ownership of subsidiaries. However, the interviews revealed that firms of all parent nationalities in extractive and high-technology activities tend to exercise tighter central control over their subsidiaries than other firms do.

U.S. extractive companies give their subsidiaries less autonomy than non-U.S. firms do, possibly reflecting a higher degree of parent ownership. As one U.S. executive noted, "As the share of minority [local] interest increases, so does entrepreneurial freedom."

The U.S. firms exercise control in a number of ways. One firm said that in principle it has no problem with diversification but that because its ties to its affiliates involve common technological procedures and products, diversification is rare. Another company explained that it has the right, through agreements with local shareholders, to veto any proposed expansion of its subsidiaries; in practice, however, it exerts its influence by "dragging its feet" when opposing a proposal to expand.

Multinationals active in high-technology manufacturing tend to exert a high degree of central control over their subsidiaries. Most do not interfere in day-to-day operations, but key decisions such as diversification require at least consultation with the parent firm and usually home-office approval. British companies in this sector appear to give their subsidiaries more freedom than other corporations do. Although they require parent-company approval on major decisions, the

British encourage their subsidiaries to move into new product lines that are profitable. Their experience has shown, however, that subsidiaries either lack the know-how to develop entirely new products or prefer to diversify into related products in which the parent company's expertise can be used.

Firms operating in fields other than high technology appear to offer their subsidiaries greater entrepreneurial freedom. Most Australian, British, and American companies said that they give their subsidiaries considerable leeway to diversify into related products within the parent firm's line. One U.S. manufacturer noted that although subsidiaries have a good deal of autonomy, the trend has been to centralize control as the parent firm grows larger. German companies said that they also tend to give their subsidiaries a great deal of autonomy, noting, however, that subsidiaries with "a considerable volume of business" usually have more influence in company decision making than smaller subsidiaries.

The Swedish companies generally exercise more control over their subsidiaries. One firm stated that it doubts its subsidiaries could have the research and development (R and D) capabilities to develop new products. Another felt that allowing subsidiaries to diversify into unrelated products would lead to risks and diseconomies for the whole corporation.

Many French manufacturers pointed out that the degree to which a subsidiary is allowed to diversify depends on a number of factors. For example, they are generally more willing to permit diversification in cases of products that do not bear the parent company's trademark.

The Japanese were particularly explicit about the areas that the parent company wants to control. These include such decisions as investing large amounts of capital, hiring top managers, and making changes in technology or product mixes. If a Japanese parent firm is a minority owner, the subsidiary has substantially more freedom.

Few parent firms in this sector are willing to allow diversification outside the company's product line. As their responses indicated, they basically see themselves as having a specific capability in particular product lines and want to be able to take advantage of the technical, managerial, and marketing skills they possess. However, when companies acquire other firms, they may take over unrelated product lines. Firms in the automotive industry believed that their subsidiaries do not have the technical capabilities to diversify. One executive stated, "Our Third World subsidiaries have enough trouble . . . being successful in the auto business." He pointed out that the closer one gets to the sale of a finished vehicle, the less leeway subsidiaries are given. But he went on to say that fewer restrictions and greater diversification might be possible in work at the component level.

Firms in the service sector accord their subsidiaries varying degrees of freedom. In general, banking concerns are restricted to banking activities. In one international bank, for example, local managers must comply with general policy and country-lending limits as determined at headquarters. In addition, each branch is bound by the rules of its host country and is subject to extensive internal and external audits. Another bank said that it gives its branch managers greater leeway in decision making but that this freedom is decreasing as the bank changes its operational structure.

Among nonbanking service firms, one parent company said that it allows diversification on a "planned basis." Another grants a high degree of freedom within the budgetary limitations set by the parent company. A third gives extensive freedom in day-to-day operations and purchasing patterns but, like all firms, requires central approval over major capital expenditures and top managerial assignments and insists that corporate policies be followed unless they contravene local law.

The interviews revealed that parent firms in all sectors overwhelmingly insist on approving their subsidiaries' major capital expenditures, including those needed for diversification, primarily because the parent normally must provide most of the funding. New, unrelated products might not be profitable, and the parent companies do not want to absorb major financial losses. Consequently, the more a subsidiary can provide its own financing for a new project, the more likely it is to receive the parent company's approval.

SEVEN

Types of Arrangements

UNBUNDLING THE
FOREIGN INVESTMENT PACKAGE

The Issues

In their dealings with subsidiaries of multinational corporations, developing countries are especially concerned about two issues: the loss of control of important sectors of the host country's economy to foreigners and the alleged excessive profits earned by transnationals through their oligopolistic combining of technology, management, marketing, and finance into a single foreign investment package.

If local enterprise, whether private or state-owned, can be encouraged to find independent sources of the various components of the foreign investment package—a process referred to as *unbundling*—would it not be possible to obtain the benefits of these resources at lower cost while retaining control of the enterprise in indigenous hands? Japan is often cited as a model for Third World nations because it has historically resisted direct foreign investment while successfully acquiring foreign technology and other resources for a fee.

The developing countries' efforts to secure unbundled foreign investment have been most successful in the natural resource field, where it has, in one form or another, become the rule rather than the exception. Among the types of arrangements that have been adopted, particularly in petroleum, are service contracts, production-sharing agreements, and technical assistance agreements. In some cases, the foreign enterprise assumes all or most of the front-end risk as well as the major responsibility for management and control. To what extent is the difference between the unbundled arrangements and the traditional concession agreement largely formal despite the new emphasis on the host country as owner and the multinational corporation as contractor?

Outside the resource field, the scope for unbundling has yet to be demonstrated. For example, to what extent are transnational manufacturing firms willing to offer their various capabilities for sale to foreign firms through licensing arrangements?

The Responses

The opinions of multinational corporations on unbundling depend largely on the individual company's philosophy and its subsidiaries' experiences in particular host countries. Only the most general statements can be made about the consistency of responses by industry group or by home country.

The developing countries' desire for unbundling has had its greatest and most immediate impact in the resource field. Extractive companies, though reluctant to enter into nontraditional arrangements, are more willing to do so than manufacturing firms, especially those engaged in high-technology activities. This greater willingness may be due partially to a recognition of the special host-country sensitivity regarding foreign ownership of natural resources and partially to the lesser flexibility of extractive companies in choosing the countries in which to invest. One extractive firm reported that the trend toward unbundling was strong ten years ago but that today host countries prefer to obtain the foreign investment package from a single source.

Only one extractive company said that it would refuse to participate in an unbundled venture. Several others expressed reservations about doing so because of the inefficiencies of "patchwork technology" and a loss of control over quality and performance. However, when companies agree to an unbundled arrangement such as a management contract, they generally insist that it be not only financially attractive but also long term. Many companies are currently operating under such contracts on a fee-for-technical-services and/or production-sharing basis.

High-technology manufacturing companies gave mixed responses regarding both pressures to unbundle and their willingness to do so. There was a rough division between U.S. and non-U.S. firms concerning pressure to unbundle. Most non-U.S.-based high technology firms had not discerned a desire on the part of host countries to purchase separate components of the investment package. In contrast, nearly all the U.S. firms reported that they have faced the demand for unbundled investment, and most maintained that the desire for this pattern of investment is widespread among developing countries. However, one company insisted that the pattern is not common outside of the countries of the Andean Pact. Another stated that most host countries want the multinational to retain some equity investment and share the risk because of the high-technology nature of the product.

On the whole, high-technology manufacturers indicated that they are either unwilling or reluctant to unbundle their investment in most of its forms. Only three firms were basically unequivocal in their willingness to cooperate in selling parts of the investment package, especially technology. Six companies were adamant in their refusal to consider unbundling. The remaining transnationals expressed a variety of reservations about unbundled arrangements, although many reported that they have licensed technology, worked under management contracts, or at least shared equity ownership.

Many companies felt that technology cannot be sold as a discrete transaction because it is inseparable from other elements of the package, such as management. Because the nature of high-technology production changes on the basis of ongoing research and development in the home country, there is also the problem of what technology is being sold. For example, one U.S. firm has been accused of selling obsolete technology. Another consideration is the maintenance of quality control. Most companies refuse to permit the use of brand names, trademarks, or logos that are identified with certain standards of quality. Two U.S. firms also mentioned that they did not wish to help establish their own competitors.

Another reason why manufacturing companies are reluctant to unbundle is insufficient remuneration. Several firms argued that developing countries simply do not have an appreciation of the costs of developing technology as an ongoing operation. Because host countries regard the costs of technology as already sunk, they are seldom willing to offer reasonable fees for its transfer. Companies also asserted that "one-shot deals" are usually not attractive because of the necessary investment of their people's time. The return to the company on the scarce time of highly skilled employees is substantially reduced when they are involved in setting up turn-key operations or providing other types of one-shot technical assistance. Nevertheless, several firms expressed a willingness to sell technology or other components of the investment package if the particular arrangements for doing so are sufficiently profitable.

In contrast, no clear distinction between U.S.-based and non-U.S.-based multinationals emerged among other manufacturing companies responding to this question. French companies generally agreed that developing countries do look for an unbundled investment package. Among the Australian, Japanese, and Swedish firms, opinions on the prevalence of the desire for an unbundled investment package were fairly evenly divided. British firms generally believed that it is not yet a widespread issue, although, again, the Andean Pact countries were mentioned as indicating an increasing wish to separate the acquisition of new technology from the investment of capital. About half of the U.S.-based companies felt that a general desire exists in developing countries to unbundle the classical foreign investment package; the others reported that they have experienced only sporadic pressure to unbundle.

Firms outside high-technology fields expressed differing degrees of enthusiasm about complying with a developing country's desire to unbundle the foreign investment package. Many multinationals will unbundle if the prospective profits and the degree of risk are reasonable, but they are basically reluctant to allow the use of their name, brand names, or trademarks unless they can retain control over the operations. Most, however, reported that they are prepared to build turn-key factories, make licensing agreements, give technical assistance, undertake management contracts, provide marketing consultation, or allow varying degrees of local ownership. Several U.S.-based firms even expressed a preference for some local ownership ("it helps relations with the host government") or licensing, particularly in politically unstable countries. A French company said that it has created a subsidiary that specializes in offering technological and engineering assistance to Third World countries.

Except for the problem of constantly evolving technology, the objections of companies in this category to breaking up the investment package are similar to those of high-technology manufacturing firms. "One-shot deals" were seen as financially unattractive; companies said that they are generally organized to provide the whole package; firms indicated that they are not interested in helping to establish competitors; and there was a general lack of willingness to assume the front-end financial risk. One firm that clearly refuses to unbundle asserted that its business is "true" industry, not providing equipment, financial resources, and technical expertise in separate components.

Although some of the service firms did not believe this issue to be relevant to their operations, one bank and the retail firms expressed a willingness to provide technical assistance without a direct-ownership relationship. The essential conditions they cited are adequate fees and no assumption of financial risks. Several service firms specifically mentioned operating under management contracts in countries where they hold a minority interest in the subsidiary or where the firm is not allowed direct equity participation. One respondent believed there is now *less* host-country resistance to direct entry by multinational firms in general and banks in particular.

The one aspect of this issue on which virtually all firms agreed was that of the cost to the host country. With the exception of a few of the non-U.S.-based firms, the multinationals strongly asserted that unbundling is a less efficient and more costly way of acquiring the foreign investment package. They cited several reasons: Unbundling may provide short-term gains to the developing country but would discourage long-term inputs from multinationals; financing is more readily available when foreign investors have equity participation; developing countries lack the managerial and administrative skills necessary to coordinate and effectively utilize all the components of the investment package; and technology that is unbundled may become obsolete before it is operational. One French company took exception to this view, pointing out that unbundling may result in lower costs to the host country because it encourages more effective competition among suppliers.

FINANCING OF OPERATIONS THROUGH LOCAL BORROWING

The Issues

Critics have asserted that the operations of transnationals in developing countries should not be equated with foreign investment because the corporations generally commit only a small amount of their own capital to the foreign enterprise, preferring, instead, to maximize their borrowings from local sources. Indeed, it would appear that only about one-quarter of foreign investment in manufacturing is financed directly by the parent companies. The rest is borrowed either locally or from other sources such as the Eurocurrency market or is generated by the subsidiaries themselves from retained earnings and depreciation.

The main reason that multinationals prefer local financing appears to be that it minimizes various types of risks, especially the risks of currency inconvertibility and depreciation, associated with a possible deterioration of a host country's balance of payments. Moreover, minimization of a parent company's financial stake in a foreign subsidiary reduces its exposure in case of nationalization.

However understandable the motivation for this policy, its consequences are regarded by host countries as detrimental to local enterprise. Local funds are usually in short supply in developing nations. Consequently, borrowings by foreign firms may deprive local projects of their only source of financing.

The Responses

Among all the companies interviewed, only the Japanese displayed a consistent pattern in the financing of subsidiaries. Almost all the Japanese multinationals have raised part of their equity capital locally by taking local partners.

Of the other firms, some indicated that they follow general principles in financing their Third World investments; whereas others reported that they evalute foreign commitments on a case-by-case basis. The guiding policies that the firms follow include minimizing equity participation, maximizing equity participation, centralizing financing in order to obtain the optimum debt/equity ratio for the whole corporation, using local financing when available, searching for low-cost credit, utilizing retained earnings and local borrowing for expansion after initial investment, and seeking outside partners for large investments. However, even companies that follow such general policies stated that they did not regard those rules as hard-and-fast. For example, an extractive company noted that although it prefers minimizing its equity participation, host governments occasionally require a conservative debt/equity ratio or the provision of 100 percent of risk capital during exploration stages.

German companies appear to prefer higher equity-to-debt ratios for their Third World subsidiaries than they maintain for affiliates located in Germany. They argued that this policy improves a foreign subsidiary's creditworthiness and ability to expand. Regardless of the amount of equity held, however, most firms of all nationalities expressed an interest in retaining management control over their subsidiaries because it facilitates borrowing in international as well as in local financial markets.

With few exceptions, multinationals have raised capital from local sources. Some firms share equity in their subsidiaries by taking on one or two local partners or permit shares in subsidiaries to be held more widely by individual local investors. More frequently, however, companies borrow from local financial sources.

Extractive firms appear to rely the least on local borrowing. This is because most developing countries do not have capital markets capable of providing the large sums required for extractive operations. As one company pointed out, "The only source which might have sufficient capital for our projects is host governments, but participation by these governments is neither assured nor necessarily advantageous."

German and American manufacturing firms are less inclined to seek local equity financing than other transnationals in that sector. In contrast, British and French manufacturers generally prefer to borrow as much capital locally as possible. In some cases, this practice is intended to create a sense of identification with the host country; in others, it is simply designed to avoid foreign exchange risks. Although the trend to local financing is not so strong among other transnationals, almost all raise at least some short-term working capital locally. Many of the Australian manufacturing firms seek local equity participation but do only a limited amount of borrowing locally.

With the exception of the banking industry, service-sector firms may raise both equity and loan capital from local sources. In the banking industry, the equity capital requirements of subsidiaries are generally quite small. Host-country laws may specify capital requirements (such as holding a certain amount of U.S. or local government securities within the host country) or quasi-equity requirements (such as holding net assets in the host country). Because the purpose of these requirements is usually cosmetic, they are typically fairly modest. The banks viewed their function as "mobilizing" local capital and making it available for borrowers, including local industry, rather than as "borrowing" locally.

The chief reason for using local sources of financing is the minimization of risk, particularly foreign exchange risk (i.e., inconvertibility and depreciation of host-country currencies). Several companies were careful to point out that although they borrow locally to avoid such risks, it is not their intention to profit from exchange rate fluctuations and that there are strict company policies prohibiting speculation. A few multinationals use local equity financing to lessen the risk of nationalization. Other reasons cited are supplementing the amount of capital exportable from the home country; creating a sense of identification with the host country; financing capital costs, such as construction, that require local currency; establishing good relationships with local bankers; and maximizing financial leverage. Moreover, local money is sometimes cheaper.

Although inflation favors a debtor position, several U.S. firms pointed out that in some countries tight money markets and high interest rates preclude local financing. In addition, local capital is frequently not available for long-term loans; this is especially true in Latin America. In these cases, multinationals commonly turn to a third source such as the Eurocurrency market.

German-based transnationals took the position that a high degree of parent-company equity investment is desirable not only because of the limited availability of local capital but also because it establishes an adequate base for the repatriation of profits in those countries where repatriation limits are related to a company's equity investment.

Virtually all the interviewed firms agreed on one major point: Their use of local loan capital does not deprive host-country enterprises of financial resources. Most companies maintained that host-government regulations are more than adequate to prevent deprivation. Others said that even if appropriate government legislation did not exist, their borrowings are so limited that the problem does not arise. A British firm and many German companies speculated that multinationals, by virtue of the evidence of their own investments in various host countries, have actually increased the supply of funds available for local firms by bolstering the confidence and willingness of foreign banks and other financial institutions to lend to domestic ventures. Several corporations also noted that because of limitations on profit repatriation, they have spare funds that they invest in both short- and long-term projects within the host country. These funds are, in turn, made available to others and thus actually increase local financial resources.

Although an Australian firm stated that "by seeking funds from local sources we have fostered and contributed to the development of local [financial] markets," other Australian companies felt that they may "possibly" be depriving locals of financing to a "very limited extent."

One firm pointed out that banks frequently prefer lending to transnationals because they are better credit risks. A small minority of the American firms was fairly certain that transnationals' borrowings are depriving locals of financing, although they, too, noted the banks' preference for lending to multinationals. However, other U.S. companies insisted that local enterprises frequently have greater access to local financing than multinationals do because of various host-country regulations and that host governments would not let a situation arise in which multinationals would deprive indigenous firms of financing.

Many transnationals recognized that where funds are limited, they may have a competitive advantage, but few believed that it is a serious problem. Several proposals were offered to help deal with whatever difficulties do arise, including limiting local borrowing by foreigners and establishing exchange rate guarantees for foreign currencies brought into the host country. However, one firm felt that in order to avoid discouraging foreign investment, no restrictions should be placed on local borrowing.

Although individual transnationals said that their local borrowings are too limited to have an impact on host-country industry, the aggregate borrowing of all transnationals may represent a substantial proportion of total borrowing in the local market. At the same time, however, they pointed out that their aggregate operations may help to increase local financial resources. Moreover, the impact of the use of local financial resources by transnationals is likely to vary from country to country, depending on the scale and form of borrowing and the size and structure of local financial markets. The net effect on local entrepreneurs is therefore difficult to measure and is probably a matter that individual companies are not in a position to assess.

JOINT VENTURES

The Issues

Transnational enterprises have traditionally preferred to establish subsidiaries that are wholly owned in order to ensure centralized management and decision making and to avoid diluting their equity returns. Developing countries, on the other hand, prefer and are increasingly requiring foreign-owned subsidiaries to take on local partners, primarily in order to strengthen the local economy's control over foreign firms.

However, the postwar trend toward a higher proportion of local own-ership of foreign affiliates may reflect not only more stringent host-government requirements but also a growing recognition by transna-tionals of the advantages of joint ownership. Local partners not only may convey a better national image for the firm but also may provide such benefits as valuable government contacts and local marketing knowl-edge and connections.

Among the questions raised by local ownership requirements are whether they deter the establishment of foreign subsidiaries or reduce the flow of managerial and technical resources once the subsidiary has been established; whether there are ways of making the required local participation more acceptable to the foreign companies; whether the host government should play a role in the choice of local partners and in de-termining the composition of the management of foreign-owned subsid-iaries; and the extent to which transnationals can reduce the onus of for-eign investment by operating as joint ventures with other foreign firms as well as with local interests.

The Responses

Although few transnationals prefer local equity participation in their subsidiaries, they are increasingly willing to accommodate to host gov-ernments' insistence on joint ventures. Acceptance of joint ventures is highest among the extractive and service companies and among firms other than those based in the United States and Germany.

With one exception, the extractive firms did not see local equity par-ticipation as a deterrent to investment. Non-U.S.-based extractive com-panies actually prefer this type of arrangement as long as the parent cor-poration retains effective control. A European firm pointed out, how-ever, that much depends on the nature of the venture. In a mining operation, a large proportion of local ownership is acceptable; but in the manufacture of finished products, a higher degree of central managerial control is required, and therefore local participation is less attractive.

American extractive companies indicated that they are less favorably inclined toward joint ventures in developing countries than other firms are, although only one flatly refused to enter into such arrangements be-cause of past experiences. Other American resource firms cited such concerns as profitability, efficiency, the "good business judgment" of local partners, and the location of the subsidiary as important in deter-

mining the degree to which the requirement of local equity participation
may deter the establishment of foreign subsidiaries or reduce the flow of
managerial and technical resources once a subsidiary has been established. One company explained that its attitude toward joint ventures is
evolving from a historical desire to own 100 percent of operations. At
present, those in the company who regularly deal with Third World nations consider joint ventures less risky than those without such experience do. The firm said that it has increasingly fewer "hang-ups" about
local participation and a growing willingness to "roll with the punches."

Among manufacturing companies, Japanese and French firms on the
whole said that they have had few problems with joint ventures with local entrepreneurs; the French have found that local equity participation
eases integration into the host-country environment. Among manufacturing firms based in other countries, opinions were more diversified.
Most manufacturers participate in joint ventures with varying degrees of
enthusiasm, although only two indicated that they willingly accept a minority equity position. German firms prefer wholly owned subsidiaries
because these generally assure more efficient operations and uniform
management and provide security for technological know-how. However, they will accept local partners if necessary. The Australian group
as a whole argued that requirements for local equity participation have
less effect on the initial investment decision than such factors as the possibility of earning an acceptable rate of return.

Firms producing high-technology goods are slightly more hesitant
than other manufacturers to engage in joint ventures. American and British firms are generally the most reluctant to share in equity ownership.
Fully half of this group said that they consider a requirement for local
equity participation a serious deterrent to direct foreign investment in
developing countries. One British company explained that this is particularly true if the parent firm is not allowed a majority holding. In explaining their hesitancy to take on local partners, several U.S. firms
pointed to the difficulty of accepting the "normal business practices" of
certain local businessmen. Several American and German companies
also pointed out that local business interests frequently look for "quick
returns" from projects; for example, they may seek dividends in a situation in which the transnational would prefer to reinvest local earnings.

Companies that did not regard local equity participation as a deterrent
expressed reservations about holding less than a controlling percentage
of the equity. Retention of control is a key condition, particularly in or-

der to maintain product quality, business integrity, efficiency of operations, and control over brand names and know-how.

Like the extractive firms, multinationals that have service subsidiaries in the Third World displayed a fair degree of willingness to enter into joint ventures. Several companies expressed a specific preference for wholly owned subsidiaries but said that if local participation requirements are not "excessive," they do not consider such conditions deterrents either to the establishment of a subsidiary or to a continued flow of resources. Indeed, one firm noted that "the need to recognize requirements of this kind is among the facts of contemporary life which have to be accepted if you want to operate in the modern world."

Most firms offered suggestions on how to make local equity participation more acceptable to transnational corporations, but no single pattern emerged, and the proposals frequently conflicted with each other. A recurrent theme was the need to maintain management control over the subsidiary. One firm suggested that if majority ownership is not possible, two classes of shares (i.e., voting and nonvoting) should be used so that the parent company can maintain some degree of management control even though it holds a minority of the equity. Others said that they prefer having many shareholders so that the company's minority holding is, in fact, the controlling interest or simply using a management contract. The desire for control pertains especially to production and quality, maintenance of trade names, and protection of patents and know-how. As long as the multinationals are allowed to control these elements, most are willing to share equity participation, and many are amenable to holding substantially less than a majority interest.

A second important proposal, mentioned especially by British firms, is that the sale of shares, whether to one or two local partners or to numerous individual shareholders, should be on a fair commercial basis and that the proceeds from the sale should be remittable to the home country. In the case of prescribed or negotiated divestiture schemes, the Japanese in particular were quite specific about acceptable terms. These include a minimum elapsed time prior to divestment so that the parent company is allowed to realize some profit from its investment, guaranteed remittance of the proceeds from the transferred equity shares, technical assistance fees and similar payments to parent firms, replacement of parent-company loan guarantees with local guarantees, and the freedom to select the local partners. However, several non-Japanese firms specifically stated that prescribed divestiture would rule out new investment on their part.

Among firms not based in Japan, many also stressed the necessity of the right to select the local partner. Some would designate a "well-established" local enterprise rather than "individual, fragmented shareholders"; other companies believed direct public ownership is more desirable. An Australian corporation suggested the establishment of "national investment companies funded by local governments which can purchase shares on behalf of indigenous people." A U.S. company said that it would prefer to sell stock to employees and have profit-sharing plans.

A number of other steps that would make local participation more attractive were mentioned. Several German firms suggested that local investors should be permitted to buy stock in the parent company so that they would become concerned with the profitability of the whole firm. An extractive firm noted that the willingness of the government to "pay up" its equity share in advance, instead of waiting for the venture to turn a profit, would be extremely helpful. Another company suggested deferring required domestic investment by locals until after the tenth year of production and allowing the local participants' share of prior costs to be recovered from their share of production. A manufacturer proposed changes in home-country accounting laws so that subsidiaries which are less than 50 percent owned by the parent company could still be consolidated. Another suggested that host governments offer tax incentives for increased local participation. In general, multinationals would find local participation more acceptable in a politically mature and hospitable investment environment.

Not surprisingly, most of the firms argued that host governments should play little or no role in the selection of subsidiary management personnel. Although many were sympathetic to the idea of utilizing host-country nationals in senior managerial positions in countries where competent candidates are to be found, most said that they believe the selection of individual employees is well outside the host government's legitimate prerogatives.

In general, American firms maintained that any government intervention in such matters is inappropriate; it is also regarded as unnecessary because most corporations prefer to employ host-country nationals when possible, recognizing the high cost of maintaining nonlocal personnel overseas. In addition, many transnationals have their own goals for the employment of nationals and thus resent further pushing by host-country governments.

Non-U.S.-based firms indicated greater willingness to acquiesce to an extremely limited host-government role in the selection of management. The Japanese suggested that except for those enterprises for which local government provides equity and/or loan capital, the government role should be limited to overall guidance and specific advice when requested, but only to the extent that it is relevant to national policy interests or objectives. Other non-U.S. firms believed that it is appropriate for the host government to establish specific goals for the employment of nonlocal personnel and of nationals in top-level management positions. However, the firms taking this position generally insisted on the right, indeed the necessity, to use home-country personnel initially and the importance of not being pushed too rapidly into indigenization. African countries were frequently cited as examples where conflicts over this issue have occurred. Two firms noted that in joint ventures in which the host government has equity participation, it is appropriate for the government to be represented on the board of directors and to approve but not to appoint the subsidiary's manager.

Only a few corporations took a position on whether joint ventures with other transnationals reduce the political and psychological burden of foreign investment. Manufacturers generally maintained that this type of joint venture is not particularly successful at relieving the onus, although a few reported that they do participate in such operations. Some believed that collaboration is not beneficial because their product lines are too specific; others objected to joining with their competitors. One company said that it would avoid such arrangements because of the antitrust implications, and another noted that "even in joint ventures with other multinationals, we would still be the gringos."

In contrast, several firms in the resource field argued that joint ventures with other transnational corporations are beneficial to both the country and the companies involved. Under such arrangements, the host country may feel less susceptible to foreign political influence and may improve its creditworthiness in a number of countries, and the companies are less likely to be targets of "nationalistic anger" and more likely to have an opportunity to spread the financial obligations and risks. One of the non-U.S. firms also suggested that inviting companies that are users of the subsidiary's output to participate in the venture can also be beneficial; such an arrangement can, for example, reduce marketing risks.

TAKEOVERS

The Issues

Almost a third of foreign subsidiaries in developing countries have been established through the acquisition of going businesses.[1] Developing countries tend to frown on such acquisitions, regarding them as alienating the domestic economy without providing offsetting benefits and, in some cases, as being intended to reduce competition and increase the dominant position of the foreign affiliate.

On the other hand, foreign firms rarely take over a local company simply for the purpose of continuing its operations as before. New products may be introduced and old equipment overhauled. Some special foreign capability in design, engineering, or production may be combined with the local company's knowledge and skill in distribution in the local market. As a result of such greater efficiency, prices may go down rather than up.

Host governments' policies on foreign acquisitions tend, therefore, to tread a delicate course between encouraging the growth of indigenous enterprise and allowing for the advantages often brought by transnationals in terms of technological and organizational innovation and economies of scale. The issues are whether and in what way acquiring a local company through a takeover affects its subsequent operation. How do the operations of such a business compare with those of a new firm?

The Responses

Most transnationals said that they have had little experience in acquiring existing local firms in developing countries. This response is borne out by the data provided by the firms. Extractive firms and high-technology manufacturers pointed out that few indigenous firms are active in their fields and that therefore few companies would be desirable acquisitions. Several multinationals engaged in manufacturing said that

[1] Raymond Vernon, *Storm Over the Multinationals: The Real Issues* (Cambridge, Mass.: Harvard University Press, 1977), p.72.

if they do take over an existing operation, it is frequently a subsidiary of another multinational, rather than a locally owned firm.

Transnationals with experience in takeovers have conflicting views about the comparative merits of acquisitions and new starts. Many companies said that they prefer newly established subsidiaries. They explained that when an existing firm is acquired, it is often difficult to resolve differences in areas such as technology, work and employment patterns, and marketing techniques. It is also easier to retain control over new starts. One corporation found itself facing "too much local interference from vendors or employees with old loyalties" when it bought an existing company.

Several European and Australian firms argued, however, that acquiring a going concern can be preferable if the company appears to be, or has the potential of quickly becoming, sound. An acquisition may reduce start-up costs and help to avoid the creation of excess capacity in the host country. Moreover, where host governments limit overall industrial capacity in a product, firms that want to manufacture locally must purchase local businesses.

A number of companies pointed to the limited opportunities to acquire economically healthy businesses. Several American, British, and Australian firms noted that developing countries generally oppose takeovers of firms that are *not* weak or failing. One U.S. company reported that it met little resistance to its takeovers because the businesses in question were in trouble. On the other hand, one bank ultimately abandoned an attempt to acquire a profitable local bank, largely because of host-government interference. An executive of another U.S. firm noted that where there is local competition, the multinational is likely to run into opposition regardless of whether it enters the market through a takeover or through a new venture. Two French companies said that they have been pressured by host governments to acquire ailing local firms. Having done so, one company found that after several years it was accused of "neocolonialist control" over a sector of the local economy.

Multinationals said that when they do take over a business, the host country benefits from the infusion of capital, technology, and managerial, marketing, and technical skills. If the acquired firm is unsound, the country may gain through the prevention of certain dislocations associated with business failures; the parasitic effects of the weak firm are also eliminated. Companies asserted that in the end, an acquisition may become a more efficient operation, benefiting the developing country in such ways as increased employment opportunities, upgraded skills, and potentially lower prices for locally produced goods.

In summary, although Third World countries express the fear that acquisitions of local firms by multinational corporations may reduce competition and lead to alienation of the local economy, the transnationals did not see these problems as important. The firms regarded host-government regulations as capable of controlling any problems that might arise. Although many companies would prefer no limits on their equity participation in local business, they have learned to live with such regulations.

EIGHT

Transfer of Technology

ADAPTATION OF PRODUCTS AND PROCESSES
TO LOCAL CONDITIONS

The Issues

Developing countries have asserted that local affiliates of multinational corporations produce inappropriate products. Too sophisticated, too highly designed, and too elaborately packaged to meet the needs of the poor masses, such products cater largely to the consumption demands of the elite. It is sometimes observed, however, that undesirable consumption patterns may in a fundamental sense be more a reflection of an existing uneven distribution of wealth, income, and privilege in developing countries than of the effects of the activities of foreign firms. The practical issues are the extent of the phenomenon of inappropriate products and what may be done to remedy it.

A related and perhaps more important issue is the appropriateness of the production processes used by foreign firms. In particular, are they excessively capital-intensive in relation to the abundance of cheap labor in developing countries? The Third World countries say that the effect in such cases is to intensify the employment problem, aggravate inequalities of income, worsen the balance of payments by excessive importation of capital equipment, and even bias the output toward excessively sophisticated products.

Again, the practical considerations are the extent to which corporations now adapt their products and processes to host-country conditions and the steps that can be taken by multinationals to encourage greater adaptation, including centralized arrangements for the development of more appropriate products and processes.

The Responses

The modification by transnationals of products and processes to reflect differing host-country circumstances is dependent on many variables, including the type of product and technology, the social and economic situation of the particular country, and the individual company's view of how its subsidiaries can function most efficiently and profitably over the long term. In general, fewer transnationals appear willing to adapt their products than to modify their processes.

Product adaptation is likely to be greatest among manufacturers of consumer goods. Besides making modifications to reflect variations in tastes, customs, and climatic and geographic conditions, companies commonly alter their products to take advantage of local raw materials. Multinationals may find it cheaper and more convenient to use indigenous resources than to import materials, or they may be forced by local-content requirements to use local inputs.

Few corporations believed that their use of locally available resources results in a reduction of quality in the goods produced. In fact, several insisted that they use local raw materials only if those materials meet stringent quality specifications. One manufacturer said that it makes no attempt to appeal to a low-income mass market by lowering the quality and prices of its products. "On the contrary, we respond to income growth by offering products to people ascending the consumer-products 'ladder.' "

Many transnationals make no more than minor modifications in their goods. According to a French and a British firm, the appeal of their products is precisely that they are standardized goods with a reputation for uniform quality. Many pharmaceutical companies maintained that they have little scope for adaptation because drugs are the result of costly research and depend on high standards of quality for medical effectiveness. These companies cannot cut corners; to do so would hurt them abroad, and any resulting bad publicity would be damaging to their public image at home.

Other multinationals are concerned with maintaining product uniformity because the interchangeability of parts and equipment is critical for a servicing network. In the automotive and heavy-machinery industries, for example, minor changes may be made, and accessories may vary, but the basic product is standardized to facilitate servicing on a worldwide basis. One firm noted that since it faces an international rather than a country-specific demand, it prefers to train service personnel, rather than to simplify its product.

Market scale and cost considerations are also important factors affecting product adaptation. Companies are not likely to develop a new product or modify an existing one unless they believe that the market is large enough to permit recovery of costs.

Unlike most transnationals, Japanese-based corporations are generally willing to tailor their products to local conditions but in practice do little in the way of process modification. The design of plants and processes is generally drafted by the parent firm. In spite of the relatively low cost of labor in Third World countries, processes similar to those used in Japan are used by subsidiaries, primarily because of the lower cost per unit of output and the greater assurance of high standards of quality.

Most transnationals from other home countries modify their processes to some extent. Indeed, the past experience of one American company indicates that such adaptation may be of critical importance to the success of its subsidiaries' operations. In Latin America, where four subsidiaries used the same technology employed in the United States, two of the subsidiaries went bankrupt, and one ran its machinery only three days a year. British firms usually stressed that the process variations they make are generally matters of degree and that the methods of production are not radically different from those used at home.

The expected scale of output, labor skill levels, and the availability and quality of local inputs, subcontractors, transportation, and communication facilities may all lead to adaptations. However, the most common reason given for changing production processes is to take advantage of comparatively cheap labor. One firm, for example, stated that it profitably employs about 1,000 people in the Philippines; whereas in Australia it uses about one-third that number in the same-size operation.

The switch to more labor-intensive methods of production may or may not be the result of conscious company policy; for example, many firms want to use more labor in packaging their products. Others stated that their use of additional labor is the result of changes in plant design. Where rapid assembly techniques cannot be used because of a low output volume, a company may decide to substitute slower manual pro-

cesses. For example, welding may be done by hand rather than by ma-
chine. Some American manufacturers felt that there is still scope for
more reduction in the capital-intensive nature of many of their Third
World operations. They said that the failure to substitute labor for capital was partly the result of the "myopic" vision of U.S. managers who
are accustomed to automated processes.

Labor-intensive industries have generally found it easier to adapt their
processes to use more host-country labor; whereas capital-intensive industries believed that the level of technology places greater constraints
on the ability to substitute labor for capital. Extractive firms find it
difficult to adapt their methods in the exploration, production, and
refining stages, although a mining company may occasionally use a
pick-and-shovel method for separating ore in place of a more capital-
intensive process. Pharmaceutical companies find that their ability to
use more labor is limited to the final packaging stage. An electronics
firm stated that although its technical processes in the manufacturing of
components are kept uniform, final assembly can more readily be
adapted to reflect local skill levels and the availability of low-cost labor.
It noted that "the labor-intensity of certain production processes made us
go abroad in the first place."

Many transnationals pointed out that the apparent low cost of host-
country labor is deceptive, noting that skill levels and productivity
in many developing countries are also low. In such cases, companies
may be inclined to use more capital-intensive, automated production
processes in order to ensure quality, uniformity, and dependability
of output. Moreover, automated processes may be preferred because
they often require less skill than more labor-intensive methods of production do.

Firms also alter their processes and plant designs to reflect the scale of
the market. Companies outside the high-technology area have greater
flexibility in reducing the size of their operations. In contrast, several high-
technology firms explained that in order to achieve needed economies of
scale, they must build plants of a particular minimum size.

Many transnationals pointed out that host-country policies have themselves created obstacles to developing appropriate products and processes. In fact, Third World countries frequently demand the most
sophisticated products and technologies. For example, one high-
technology company said that it would be willing to switch to more labor-intensive equipment by using fifty-year-old machinery, but it has

found most developing countries unreceptive to this idea. Another firm reported that it tried to market a simplified product designed specifically for developing countries, only to find that the countries "would have nothing to do with it."

Host-country labor policies also appear to promote more capital-intensive processes. Although corporations readily accommodate to host-country employment regulations, restrictions on the right to dismiss employees make them more inclined in certain cases to make more extensive use of automated methods of production.

The interviews revealed widespread agreement on one point: The various "capital-cheapening" policies of host governments, such as overvalued exchange rates and tariff concessions on imports of new equipment, are not the major considerations in the decision to use capital-intensive processes. Only a handful of firms, particularly German-based corporations, said that such policies as investment tax credits and low-cost loans for capital equipment are significant in the choice of a production process. Most transnationals stated that their choice of process is based mainly on technical considerations, the anticipated scale of output, the availability of skilled labor, and the need to ensure high standards of quality. The British, for example, normally install the most modern plant possible because they are not experienced in the efficient use of labor-intensive plants. However, it is unclear to what extent the view that capital-cheapening policies are of little import reflects a failure to give explicit consideration to such policies when weighing the costs and benefits of alternative methods. At the margin, these policies undoubtedly do contribute to the choice of capital-intensive processes.

French-based transnationals have generally found that the policies of host countries are evolving. Whereas developing countries once supported the use of the most modern, capital-intensive technology, they are now increasingly concerned with technologies that result in higher profits to the subsidiary and lower costs to local consumers.

Although many companies modify their products and/or methods of production to reflect the differing host-country circumstances, most have no centralized arrangements for considering these adaptations before technology is transferred. The Japanese firms are the major exception in this respect; they usually send groups of experts to their subsidiaries to gain firsthand knowledge of conditions, and the experts' findings are then considered in decisions on appropriate products and processes. Nevertheless, in practice, subsidiary plant design and processes do not often deviate substantially from the standard Japanese model. Several European firms also have such arrangements. For example, one corporation has a plant that deals exclusively with the problems of starting and sustaining industrial activities in the Third World. Another has a special department that adapts investment projects to use less sophisticated production techniques.

Among the remaining transnationals, methods for evaluating adaptations vary greatly. Most American manufacturers, especially those not in high-technology fields, have some type of formal arrangement for considering technological adaptations. Regardless of the nationality of the parent company, transnationals that do not have central channels to consider adaptations may still do so on a project-by-project basis or may allow their subsidiaries to make on-the-spot changes appropriate to local markets.

Most British and German firms said that they consider local adaptations and give advice to their subsidiaries on an informal basis. The subsidiaries of most Swedish transnationals work out their own adaptations, although the parent company may assist in carrying out the design. However, one Swedish firm has a central staff charged with developing processes specifically for use in Third World countries. The Australian companies were evenly divided; about half have formal, home-office divisions for considering appropriate adaptations. The French generally have no such arrangements.

LICENSES AND PATENTS

The Issues

Many developing countries regard the purchase of technology through licensing arrangements, without equity participation by the foreign owner of the technology, as a highly desirable way of bringing about a transfer of technology while minimizing loss of control of economic activity. At the other end of the spectrum, wholly owned subsidiaries may not pay separately for technology through royalties and technical fees because the benefits of technology accrue to the parent firm in the form of the subsidiaries' earnings and the dividends paid to the parent. In the case of partial equity ownership by the transnational, the separate payment of royalties and fees for parent-company technology is quite common.

The host countries' principal concerns with respect to the purchase of technology, whether patented or unpatented, are the price charged and the restrictive conditions attached to the licensing agreements. There is a tendency to regard technology as being sold under monopolistic or oligopolistic conditions and hence as being overpriced, Moreover, the royalties paid for technology are seen as excessive in relation to the transfer costs because the expenses incurred by the transnational in developing it have already been sunk.

Perhaps the most serious concern, however, relates to the restrictive clauses commonly included in licensing agreements. Among those deemed most objectionable are clauses obliging the licensee to purchase materials, components, or equipment from the licensor (often at prices considered excessive), limitation of sales to the domestic market or to designated foreign markets, and grant-back provisions (i.e., provisions that give the licensor all rights to improvements).

The principal issues are the extent of such practices, the corporations' reactions to host-government efforts to control or approve technology licensing agreements, and their views on how host-country governments can most effectively prevent the abuses associated with the transfer of both patented and unpatented technology.

The Responses

Transnationals engaged in extractive and service activities did not consider the issues concerning the licensing and patenting of technology significant in their operations.

In the manufacturing sector, most companies reported that they use licensing agreements and that some restrictions are usually involved. However, Swedish manufacturers and Australian high-technology firms said that licenses do not play an important role in their business.

Few multinationals that license technology require licensees to purchase raw materials or components from the licensor; often they do not have such materials to offer the licensee. However, companies producing consumer goods tend to be exceptions. In many cases, these firms either have to approve raw material purchases or require the licensee to buy them from the licensor in order to ensure consistent product quality. Some multinationals, particularly those in the food and beverage industries, *insist* that the licensee buy from them. Not only is product quality important to these companies, but "it's a matter of keeping one's recipe to oneself."

German transnationals commonly reserve the right to sample a licensee's output at random. This requirement is used in combination with restrictions on the purchase of raw materials and components to ensure product quality.

The most common restrictive clauses in licensing agreements are limits on sales to home markets or designated foreign markets and grant-back provisions. Although most transnationals provide for grant-backs in licensing agreements, several said that unless the licensee is relatively sophisticated (e.g., a subsidiary of another corporation), virtually all the technological flow will be from the licensor to the licensing corporation.

Firms that place formal or informal restrictions on a licensee's exports usually do so to prevent competition with other subsidiaries or licensees of the same parent company. But when a host country is no longer willing to permit such restrictions, companies will often license anyway and accept competition from affiliates and licensees. However, several French and other European companies noted that their subsidiaries are usually established as a result of import-substitution policies and that competitive exporting among subsidiaries is therefore highly unlikely. In comparison with other firms, American multinationals are at a disadvantage when trying to restrict exports. American antitrust legislation, applied extraterritorially, prohibits most attempts by U.S. multinationals to include such restrictions in licensing agreements with nonaffiliated companies.[1]

Although most manufacturers use licensing agreements, few believed that patent monopolies per se are particularly important to the transfer of technology to developing countries. One U.S. executive argued that patents are more important in form than in substance; that is, there is some image value in holding many patents. Protection of know-how and trademarks is crucial, however. Companies that use technologies involving a large engineering component asserted that the capacity to use and build around the technology is critical. In areas such as consumer products, trademarks and brand names represent a company's reputation and must therefore be protected as much as possible. Protection is achieved primarily through strict quality controls for products bearing the licensor's name.

[1] According to current interpretation of U.S. law and practice, agreements between a parent company and independent firms containing such restraints as the fixing of prices or the allocation of markets are generally considered illegal if they restrain U.S. trade. However, a parent company may fix prices or allocate markets for subsidiaries that it fully controls.

Although most of the interviewed corporations played down the significance of patents, the chemical and pharmaceutical firms generally said that they are quite important. For these companies, actual production costs tend to be relatively low, but research costs often form a major portion of total expenses, so that patent monopolies are "absolutely vital" in ensuring the recovery of such costs. The decision to invest is, in the eyes of one firm, definitely affected by the patent regulations and practices in a given country. Another company said that host-country import-substitution policies, which create markets sheltered from foreign competition, often take the place of patent protection in circumstances in which foreign firms might otherwise try to compete on the basis of pirated technology.

That developing countries do not recognize the real costs of technology was a point repeatedly stressed by the interviewed firms. If technology were properly regarded as a flow rather than as a stock, the transnationals insisted, licensing fees would not appear excessive. The revenue stream must be sufficient not only to cover sunk costs but also to sustain the continued generation of technological innovation.

French and German companies were particularly critical of the prevailing Third World philosophy, which they said views technology as "part of the common heritage of mankind." French firms stated that this attitude is most common in Latin America, especially in Brazil. In practice, French corporations generally try to maintain the principle of royalty payments even if these are modest and must be reinvested locally. To recover its costs, one French firm requires its licensees to buy components from the parent company. German companies affirmed that restrictions on, and the taxation of, royalty payments are making it increasingly unattractive to transfer technology to developing countries.

Most companies that license technology or hold patents reported that they have experienced host-government efforts to control these arrangements. Governments usually closely monitor and are quite knowledgeable about licensing agreements. According to one executive, "They are on to all the tricks." They also show no hesitation in asking for the inclusion in licensing arrangements of conditions such as export or local-content requirements, "use it or lose it" regulations,[2] and limits on royalty rates. If the market is large and promises sufficient growth potential, transnationals may accept these conditions. But several companies as-

---

[2] Such regulations stipulate that patented technology moves into the public domain if the company holding the patent fails to use or license the technology.

serted that such conditions may result in loss of control over sales and product quality and that the restrictions therefore discourage the transfer of technology.

Multinationals criticized the weak state of patent and trademark legislation in developing countries. They explained that the regulations are typically poorly prepared or administered, which makes it difficult for some companies to protect their industrial property rights. One U.S. consumer goods firm, for example, has not even tried to register its trademark in India because in practice the protection provided by the trademark would be so weak. Several firms reported that they have had their technology pirated or their trademarks infringed upon.

Another complaint, made primarily by some of the pharmaceutical companies, is that even when patent rights are granted, their extremely short duration renders the patent useless. It takes several years to develop and market a product, by which time the patent may have elapsed. One executive believed that developing countries simply do not understand, or refuse to understand, that without sufficient patent protection, his company cannot earn a reasonable return on its investment in research and development.

Multinationals had several suggestions for controlling the abuses associated with the transfer of patented and unpatented technology: the adoption of "use it or lose it" regulations, the development by host countries of alternative technological processes, the creation of a system of "international joint review of patent monopolies," and the enactment of "fair" antitrust legislation. Most important, the corporations stressed, is the need for developing countries to avoid arbitrary decisions. A number of companies said that they can adapt to almost any policy provided it is applied consistently.

RESEARCH AND DEVELOPMENT IN THE THIRD WORLD

The Issues

Because they often regard foreign technology as inappropriate, high priced, and subject to restrictive conditions, many developing countries have sought to reduce their dependence on imports of technology by encouraging the development of an indigenous R and D capability. However, if there is no existing domestic core of R and D facilities, this effort can be extremely frustrating. Apart from the high costs, there is the brain drain, that is, the tendency of scientists and engineers to migrate from poor to rich countries not only because of higher salaries but also because of the wider contacts, more ample infrastructure of equipment and publication facilities, and other advantages.

The multinationals are alleged to have little interest in countering these tendencies by establishing R and D facilities in the Third World countries in which they operate. They are said to have shown a strong preference for locating such facilities at home or in other developed countries and for concentrating on the kinds of products and processes appropriate to their main markets in high-income countries.

The issues raised here are whether transnationals have in fact established R and D facilities in developing countries and for what reasons. Where they have not done so, under what conditions would they consider establishing such facilities? Alternatively, would multinational corporations contribute financially or technologically to a local facility sponsored by the host government, an industry association, a university, or some other institution?

The Responses

If research and development is defined to include the performance of basic research, then it is true that multinationals generally do not have R and D facilities in Third World countries. However, many firms do have local capabilities for product testing and adaptation, quality control, or technical trouble-shooting. In some developing countries, these operations have the potential for evolving into substantial R and D capabilities.

No extractive firm has established R and D facilities per se in host countries, but as one mining firm observed, each situation is unique. The organization responsible for the mining venture must have the ability to respond to the problems it faces. In one case, this involved the development of a new type of dredge. A resource-processing company noted that because of variations in ore bodies, much process development may have to be done on location rather than in the home country.

Manufacturing firms reported that they have established applied R and D and product development facilities in several developing countries where there are large or rapidly growing markets. Most of these institutions are located in Brazil and India; particular companies also mentioned Nigeria, Mexico, Saudi Arabia, and Argentina. Although in a few cases the facilities are quite substantial, most are limited to the solving of the particular subsidiary's special problems.

Among manufacturing firms, high-technology companies are the most likely to have some type of R and D capability in at least one developing country. Two companies, both operating in India, said that they have been pressured by local partners or the host government into creating indigenous R and D institutions. A Swedish transnational has a policy of doing research and development in each developing country in which it manufactures because such work "must be done close to the markets so as to appreciate special local conditions." Other manufacturing firms ageed that an indigenous R and D capability may be necessary when local conditions require substantial product development, testing, and adaptation. Several companies stated that they may establish local R and D facilities because the product line of the subsidiary deviates from that of the parent corporation.

Manufacturing firms that do little or no research and development in Third World countries generally explained their position in terms of the lack of skilled local personnel and the inadequate size of local markets. One company said that even at home it does only a limited amount of research and development and that therefore establishing such facilities abroad "does not make much sense." Several multinationals, particularly the German firms, believed that the advantages of economies of scale and the centralization of information are such that they have not established R and D facilities in foreign industrialized countries either. Japanese companies have found that the need for local research and development has not yet arisen. Finally, because some firms require that their products be engineered to uniform specifications, research and development in host countries would simply duplicate existing facilities.

Most firms without R and D facilities in developing countries would consider establishing them "when it is technically advantageous and cost-competitive." Others have determined quite exact criteria such as cutoff points for the size of markets. Some transnationals stated that they require "adequate infrastructure for conducting R and D," although specific components of that infrastructure were not named. German companies generally believed that research and development is most likely to be decentralized to countries with large internal markets or to regional common markets.

As an alternative to establishing their own R and D facilities in host countries, transnationals could contribute financially and/or technologically to local facilities, universities, and research institutions, both government-sponsored and privately owned. British and French firms were the least enthusiastic in their support for local research institutions. The few U.K. companies that provide support do so only occasionally and only on a modest scale. One French company, however, reported that it is quite active in this area. Besides contributing to all local facilities, it has established a consulting group to further the transfer of technology.

The Japanese, Swedish, and other European multinationals were evenly divided on the issue. Japanese firms generally welcome greater R and D support from the Japanese government for research facilities. Swedish transnationals that support local research facilities are all in the extractive and high-technology manufacturing areas. Other Swedish firms felt that their R and D needs are far too company-specific for the work of outside institutions to be of benefit. The other European firms generally reported that they would or do support some local research facilities.

With two exceptions, Australian companies either currently contribute to local research institutions or would consider doing so under certain conditions. One firm said that "rather than contribute funds to a government-sponsored facility, we see direct sponsorship of scholars/apprentices and specific training programs as providing a more positive contribution."

American firms overwhelmingly support local research institutions either financially or technologically or would consider doing so under certain conditions. Some companies steer away from government facilities but support university research on a selective basis. Others would provide support when the research is "highly relevant" to their operations. German transnationals also cooperate extensively with indigenous research institutions.

EMPLOYMENT LEGISLATION AND TRAINING EFFORTS

The Issues

Developing countries seek to indigenize the local operations of foreign firms as a means of exercising greater control over subsidiaries and of placing themselves in a position to pursue their industrialization goals with less dependence on foreign firms. To this end, a number of host countries have extensive legislation and regulations on employment conditions and industrial relations, for example, requirements for the training and upgrading of the labor force and limitations on the number and type of foreign nationals that may be employed. In addition, host countries commonly impose conditions designed to protect the jobs of their nationals. These measures include rules for consultation with government and employee representatives on changes in operations affecting the livelihood of employees and limitations on the right to discharge workers or to threaten, in the context of labor negotiations, to transfer an operating unit from the country.

To what extent have transnationals faced requirements of this sort, and how have they reacted? More particular issues relate to the nature and adequacy of training facilities for local employees of foreign affiliates, especially training for higher levels of management. For example, are facilities provided for home-country training of host-country nationals? Do multinationals support local or regional management training programs such as the Asian Institute of Management in Manila or the Fundação Getulio Vargas in São Paolo? Finally, to what extent are subsidiaries in developing countries headed by host-country nationals, and where they are not, under what circumstances would nationals be appointed?

The Responses

With few exceptions, multinationals said they are confronted with host-country laws and regulations governing employment practices and conditions. Most frequently, they face employment-stability laws that place stringent limitations on the right to dismiss employees. French firms were particularly concerned about limits on the use of home-country personnel. Other employment regulations mentioned were training requirements in both managerial and technical skills, ethnic-balance requirements, and a variety of mandatory social welfare contributions. One U.S. extractive firm found that in the developing countries in which it operates, the requirements are usually not formal; rather, there are social and cultural norms to which the company tries to adjust.

In all but a few cases, transnationals have had few problems in complying with these regulations. Although the rules may have prevented the most effective use of manpower, companies were usually able to adapt to the restrictions. However, German firms noted that the use of nonlocal staff is almost unavoidable if technology is to be transferred.

In several cases, firms claimed that standard company hiring and employment practices exceed the requirements of many host governments. Where host-country employment regulations differ from the corporations' employment practices, most firms have found that the requirements do not discriminate against multinationals; they generally apply equally to local and foreign-owned enterprise. Some American and British firms and, in particular, Swedish companies asserted that strict employment regulations are not unique to developing countries and that such regulations are often less onerous and less strictly enforced than those imposed by industrialized countries.

Transnationals have found that problems usually arise because the host government tries to implement requirements more quickly than is realistic or fails to state its goals clearly. In these cases, any difficulties are generally solved through negotiation. Asian countries are regarded by most of the companies as more willing to negotiate over employment requirements than African or Latin American countries are. Malaysia, however, was singled out by several firms as a country in which severe problems exist, particularly regarding ethnic-balance regulations and limits on the use of foreign personnel. At least one firm reported that it is considering withdrawing from Malaysia because of these requirements.

In most cases, transnationals take host-country employment regulations into account before investing. If they do invest, they may work around these requirements in several ways. For example, several companies said that restrictions on the right to dismiss employees encouraged them to use more capital-intensive methods of production. Others, viewing labor as an overhead cost, try to produce for inventory when sales fall off. One Swedish corporation said that it avoids discharging personnel, even though not bound by legislation in this regard, because it feels "morally obliged" not to reduce employment where no other employment opportunities exist.

All the multinationals reported that they offer a wide range of host- and home-country training programs for local managerial and technical personnel. The programs include on-the-job training, domestic and foreign university training, company-run and outside training programs in both the host and the home countries, and the use of "mature" subsidiaries as instruction centers. Companies also rotate employees among several different subsidiaries to expose them to all facets of the firm's operations. Several Swedish multinationals that use English as their official language send host-country employees to English-speaking schools or provide language training. German-based firms also offer language training for their host-country employees. Most of the corporations believed that a mixture of programs is most effective in training personnel, but the Japanese expressed a distinct preference for on-the-job training. Besides offering their own managerial training programs, many firms provide both financial and personnel support for local and regional out-company training programs such as the Fundação Getulio Vargas, the Asian Institute of Management, and the Singapore Institute of Management.

One reason transnationals provide extensive educational programs is that host-country nationals are increasingly playing key roles in management. Transnationals overwhelmingly favor the principle of local nationals managing subsidiaries. The factual data provided by the firms showed that a substantial majority of managerial positions in subsidiaries are held by nationals. Perhaps because of this fact, few firms except the French, Japanese, and some other European companies offer extensive orientation programs for home-country managerial personnel who are sent to developing countries. Companies often said that such efforts would be wasted because these people will not be in any particular Third World country for long.

Transnationals employ host-country nationals as managers because of an increased awareness of the financial and psychological costs of employing nonlocal personnel. It is very costly to transport and maintain foreign managers and their families. Moreover, foreign assignments may take an executive out of the mainstream of career development. Such an employee may feel that he has "lost out" or may become "too comfortable" abroad and be reluctant to rejoin the parent company.

Transnationals that do not use locals in management generally said that indigenous personnel are not experienced enough to run the operation. In such cases, one firm prefers to appoint a local as nominal head (president or chairman) and place an expatriate, who will run the subsidiary's operation, in the second-ranking position (chief executive officer). However, these companies do plan to promote locals as soon as it is practical to do so. As one executive stated, "When we send in a foreign manager, we hope he will do himself out of a job." Several multinationals noted that although they support the principle of locals holding important managerial posts, rotational systems for employees within the company may cause locals to be moved from their own country and replaced by third-country personnel.

LINKAGE TO THE HOST COUNTRY'S
DOMESTIC ECONOMY

The Issues

Host governments commonly assert that certain types of foreign operations have an enclave character; that is, they have few backward or forward linkages to the domestic economy. *Backward linkages* are the purchase of local inputs; *forward linkages* are the domestic use of the firm's output in further productive operations. Examples of inadequate backward linkages are the assembly of automobiles from imported components and the packaging of pharmaceuticals from imported materials. Examples of inadequate forward linkages are the export of ores or logs without further local processing into metals or plywood. The processing of imported goods for reexport illustrates both types of enclave operations.

Third World governments have made various attempts to encourage closer integration of foreign operations with the local economy. They often require progressive increases in the local value-added content of manufacturing products either within the foreign affiliate or through subcontracting to local firms. Other measures with similar objectives include prohibition of the export of materials in their raw form and positive inducements for further local processing of primary materials. Host governments would also like to see multinational corporations make greater use of local engineering and consulting firms.

To what extent have multinationals encountered efforts at this type of integration with the local economy? How effective have these efforts been in accomplishing their purpose of promoting indigenous industrialization and development?

The Responses

Transnationals draw a distinction between backward and forward linkages. Few companies have difficulties in meeting requirements, such as local-content regulations, designed to promote backward linkages. However, many transnationals, particularly the extractive firms, stated that forced forward linkages create serious problems.

Local-content requirements are enforced by host governments in various ways. Preferences for domestic value added may be given in the administration of the government's own purchases, in the granting of import licenses, or through government price controls that give credit for increased local content.

Companies have generally adapted to these requirements with relative ease, and in fact, many firms prefer using local inputs when they are available. The factual data presented by the firms indicated that transnationals generally do make good use of local inputs. In particular, most British and French corporations said that these requirements are reasonable as long as they are not pushed too far or too fast. One French manufacturer believed that instead of emphasizing the manufacture of many parts locally, a developing country should concentrate on mass-producing a few parts that could be exported; such a policy would lead to lower domestic costs and perhaps to higher foreign exchange receipts.

Several companies pointed out that local-content requirements result in increased costs for both themselves and the host countries. The Japanese as a group and some other companies have found that the requirements have lowered the product quality and profitability of some subsidiaries. A number of American firms noted that although value-added requirements are "the best thing" that developing countries can do to industrialize, the initial result is usually premium prices for processed goods.

Local-content requirements do occasionally present problems. Many manufacturers pointed to Latin American countries, particularly Mexico and Brazil, as places where local-content requirements are sometimes excessive. An Australian company established a plant in one Third World country specifically for the local processing of primary materials, but the host government imposed such heavy export duties on the finished product that the plant became uneconomical.

In general, extractive companies reported that they are facing increasing pressure to create forward linkages through the further processing of raw materials. For example, one firm described the policy of the Philippines, which, it said, ties the amount of foreign equity ownership permissible to the extent of linkages. If raw materials are exploited, foreign equity participation can be only 30 percent; if very simple first-stage processing is added, permissible equity rises to 40 percent; and if further processing is done, the proportion of foreign ownership allowed is 60 percent.

Although most extractive firms recognized that the enclave problem tends to be inherent in the resource field, none were willing to yield to host-country pressure unless the proposed downstream venture is economically viable. One company said it hesitates to become involved in further processing because of the additional heavy capital outlay that would be necessary. Reluctance to invest downstream is also based on "the rigidities introduced." Further processing of ore concentrate into more specialized materials at the point of extraction may substantially limit the market by creating an inability to meet a wide variety of shifting final demands for its products.

Extractive firms generally pointed out that requiring forward linkages in the resource field or forbidding the export of primary materials in an unprocessed form is usually not in the best interest of the host country. Except in the case of countries that have their own oil and could argue the need for refining capacity on the basis of security reasons, forced forward linkages may be economically inadvisable, particularly if they take a multinational out of its area of expertise. Several extractive firms also observed that such policies could decrease foreign investment and therefore retard economic development. More specifically, one company asserted that if one of its host countries should forbid the export of semiprocessed ore, its subsidiary would have to cease functioning. Another noted that if a particular host government had required a smelter as part of the project, the venture would not have been initiated.

Although manufacturing firms are basically unaffected by this problem, they recognized the difficulties that mandatory forward linkages in the extractive field can cause. The Japanese believed that restrictions on the export of raw materials would be certain to slow development in host countries because of the resulting capital flight or reduced capital inflow, increased competition from raw materials exports from countries that do not have such policies, and the development of substitutes. An Australian firm suggested that because "the ultimate aim of the host country must be self-processing," processing should perhaps be required on a gradual, step-by-step basis. One approach proposed by another Australian firm is that export of primary materials "be licensed and tied to a timetable for development of first-stage processing, for example, western Australia's iron ore leases." One company felt that the processing of primary products should be encouraged by "creating the right kind of stable investment climate. If this can be achieved, then most governments should consider a ban on the export of these materials." The firm also noted, however, that processing can be justified only if the processed product can compete on the world market. Finally, some manufacturers believed that although an embargo on the export of primary materials would not be beneficial, export duties on these resources may be acceptable.

One manner in which transnationals generally find it in their interest to integrate into the domestic economy is through subcontracting, and most firms reported that they do subcontract to some degree. The practice is least common among Japanese firms, although more than half of them do so. How extensively subcontracting is used in a developing country depends heavily on the technology, skills, and related industries available in that country; the nature of the product manufactured; and the host government's policies in this area.

All extractive firms subcontract, although two limit this activity to construction. The others usually farm out as much as possible, generally in the fields of maintenance and repair, transport, construction, and related services. Extractive companies whose ventures require the establishment of mining towns rely even more heavily on subcontracting in order to provide services to the towns.

After extractive firms, the high-technology manufacturers are the most extensive users of subcontracting. All these firms subcontract to some extent, with the exception of one, which refrains from doing so for security reasons. The reasons for subcontracting vary from company to company and are at times inconsistent among different firms.

Several high-technology companies subcontract extensively in order to meet local-content requirements. However, a few of them, like the extractive firms, limit their subcontracting primarily to services in such areas as plant construction and maintenance. One high-technology transnational limits assignments to individual subcontractors so that no more than 20 percent of their business is with the firm. Thus, when the corporation "hits a slump," the economic damage to the subcontractor is limited. Conversely, a European firm restricts the amount of business it does with an individual subcontractor in order to avoid becoming too dependent on a single source of supply.

Most of the other manufacturers, including all those based in the United States, subcontract to some extent. The practice is, however, frequently more limited than it is with their high-technology counterparts. Some companies subcontract for individual purchase orders for which specifications are usually provided; others maintain a more ongoing relationship with their suppliers. Frequently, the use of local firms is limited to such services as cleaning, legal advice, advertising, public relations, and product packaging.

The assistance given to subcontractors by transnational firms covers a wide range. Only two companies addressing this issue said that they provided no assistance at all. Most at least offer technical aid such as blueprints, specifications, tooling, training, quality control, and know-how. One transnational provides extensive assistance to its subcontractors with the goal of offloading the simpler, standardized, and "long-series" items that lend themselves to subcontracting. At the other extreme, some firms subcontract relatively simple parts and assemblies that have to be made to custom specifications.

In the service sector, there is a clear dichotomy between banks and retail firms. Although banks may be required to subcontract in such areas as external auditing, they generally found the question of linkages to be of little importance to their operations.

Retailers, on the other hand, may make extensive use of local sources of supply. One firm, for example, prefers to use local suppliers so long as costs are not excessive and pursues an active policy of assisting firms to establish production facilities.

NINE

Other Host-Country Policies

INVESTMENT INCENTIVES

The Issues

Investment incentives granted by the countries of the Third World fall into two broad groups: incentives to encourage industrial development regardless of the source of the investment and special inducements to attract foreign investment or particular types of it such as export-oriented industries.

Tariff or quota protection in the home market has already been discussed (see Chapter 6). Another type of general trade measure to induce investment is tariff reductions on required imports of raw materials, components, or equipment. In addition, developing countries often grant fiscal incentives of various kinds such as corporate income tax reductions or holidays, accelerated depreciation, and investment credits. Occasionally, the host country will seek to attract investment by providing the necessary infrastructure, such as roads, electric power, and housing.

A basic question raised by host-country incentives is whether they significantly increase the inflow of foreign investment. If they do, do the resulting benefits in terms of development exceed the costs?

It is sometimes alleged that incentive schemes result in mutually disadvantageous competition among developing countries to attract foreign investment. As a consequence, they tend to cancel each other out and simply raise the returns to foreign firms that would invest anyway. How can this problem best be met?

The Responses

With the exception of service-sector firms, the multinationals reported that they have generally benefited from host-country investment incentives. Tax concessions appear to be the most common; they are granted for investing in a country, agreeing to meet export targets, expanding productive capacity, and locating operations in particular geographic regions within a country. Although several firms said that Asian countries offer more incentives than other developing nations do, experience varied among the companies.

The factual data made available by the companies suggest that Japanese subsidiaries make the most extensive use of investment incentives; American affiliates are next. Subsidiaries of companies based in Europe and Australia generally receive few host-country investment incentives.

Although transnationals usually take advantage of any incentives offered by host countries, they generally do not actively seek out special inducements because such arrangements increase the visibility and vulnerability of the firms. According to an American executive, "Special deals and exceptions stick out like a sore thumb and tend to backfire." For example, tax agreements negotiated by an extractive company with various colonial authorities gave the host countries a "pittance" in terms of the total value of production. In reaction, the host governments later imposed a high production levy. "If we had had an enlightened tax policy, [the countries] would have been much less antagonistic and would have probably not imposed a levy so much in excess of their needs."

Only a handful of firms stated that special incentives have been major considerations in their investment decisions. At the margin, however, incentives can tip the balance, making a previously doubtful venture attractive. In some cases, incentives may affect where a project is undertaken but not the size of the total commitment. Incentives are frequently offered to offset disadvantages and risks inherent in investing in the Third World or as quid pro quo for some action, such as agreeing to export, that the multinational would not undertake in its own interest.

Incentives were also considered too "volatile" and "transitory." In particular, tax concessions were often found to be "illusory." Tax holidays are often given to firms during the early years of their operations, a time when they are least likely to show a profit and therefore to be able to take advantage of the incentive. In addition, as one U.S. firm pointed out, under the foreign tax credit system, it may not necessarily be to the company's advantage to pay lower taxes abroad.

Several companies did say that incentives have been important in decisions to increase their investments in developing countries. By "incentives," these companies generally meant protection from import competition.

Many transnationals did not believe mutually disadvantageous competition among developing countries in offering investment incentives to be a particularly serious problem. One U.S. executive asserted that such competition is more common among developed countries, particularly in Europe. In many cases, competition may actually be advantageous to some developing countries. Because of differences in size, stage of economic development, and political stability, certain nations have to offer incentives if they are to attract private foreign investment. According to many transnationals, it is the job of the host country to balance the costs of such policies against the net benefits of foreign investment.

Other companies said that a problem does exist. The most frequently suggested solution was some type of regional or global harmonization of incentives, perhaps in the form of a code of conduct for host countries. Several firms felt that developing countries should eliminate all incentives. Japanese companies proposed an intraregional division of labor based on the comparative advantages of the constituent countries. However, the multinationals saw only a slim likelihood that any such proposals would succeed. All would involve a loss of sovereignty for individual countries that most would find intolerable. As long as developing countries are "bidding" for a limited pool of foreign investment funds, competition in incentives will persist.

TRANSFER PRICING AND TAXATION

The Issues

A substantial proportion of a foreign subsidiary's purchases and sales are transactions with the parent firm or its other affiliates. Critics allege that the transfer prices on such transactions often diverge from the arm's-length prices that would prevail through the working of market forces if the parties to the transaction were unrelated. This divergence is said to reflect attempts to offset the effects of price-fixing and foreign exchange restrictions as well as to exploit, for company benefit and usually to the detriment of the host country, differences in taxes and other economic conditions in the various countries in which the transnational operates. For example, corporations may manipulate intracorporate import and export prices in order to shift profits from jurisdictions with high profits taxes to those with low taxes.

The principal issues raised by transfer pricing are the extent of such practices, their effects on the developing countries, and the measures that might be taken by host and home countries to monitor transfer pricing and to prevent the abuses associated with it.

The Responses

Few transnationals admitted to the use of transfers at other than arm's-length prices, and there was substantial disagreement and inconsistency in responses to questions concerning the extent and nature of these practices. Although many firms insisted that the extent of manipulative practices has been exaggerated, most claimed to "have no idea" how common non-arm's-length transfer pricing is because of a lack of "firsthand knowledge." However, several maintained that the use of special transfer prices is probably widespread.

Only a handful of companies said that they exploit transfer pricing to gain special advantage. Moreover, no firm admitted to using special transfer prices as a means of evading host-country taxes.

Several manufacturers asserted that the manipulation of transfer pricing is probably common in the extractive sector, but extractive firms argued that such practices are not possible in their industry, primarily because there are world market prices for primary products. Only one extractive company stated that it has used special prices in intracorporate transactions, and it believed this practice worked to the advantage of the host country. Transfers at other than arm's-length prices were regarded as more common among companies with a high degree of centralized control than among firms with largely autonomous, self-sufficient subsidiaries. In addition, the corporations believed that the exploitation of transfer pricing is more likely to occur in the early stages of a project, rather than when a subsidiary is well established, and in companies that feel they are being unfairly dealt with by host governments.

Some transnationals maintained that because of restrictions on payments of royalties and fees for research and development, limits on dividends, price controls on final products, or restrictions on charging administrative expenses to foreign affiliates, transfer prices need to be adjusted if business is to be conducted at a level which permits a profit to be earned. Transfer prices, they stated, are not adjusted for the purpose of avoiding local income taxes. This situation was most commonly encountered in discussion with pharmaceutical companies. Some other transnationals indicated they may use special transfer prices so as to increase profits in Third World subsidiaries to help meet their cash-flow needs and to make increased use of tax deferral.

Those transnationals that said they do not manipulate transfer prices noted that such practices are in most cases against company policy. They also claimed that not much scope is offered for special transfer pricing because little internal trading occurs, that special prices in intracorporate transactions may make products less competitive, that local shareholders would object to abusive transfer pricing, that the company's structure encourages high subsidiary profitability by considering each a "profit center," and that the benefits of non-arm's-length transfer pricing do not offset the costs involved.

To the extent that transfer pricing is used to gain special advantage, the corporations expressed a variety of opinions on what measures can be taken by host governments to prevent abuses. Although some companies believed that host countries are limited in their ability to control or monitor such practices, most stated that host governments should closely examine intracorporate transactions. Such monitoring would include examining invoices of companies that ship similar products or comparing data from different subsidiaries of a parent firm. However, a problem in monitoring transfer pricing is that the allocation of indirect and joint costs is often based on subjective considerations and can differ from company to company.

In addition, host governments should look at world market data to determine fair-market value. One transnational felt that "frontier prices" should be related to "a formula based on comparable external prices, having regard to local conditions such as customs and other levies, exchange rates, transport costs, and so on." Other suggestions included freeing the repatriation of profits and allowing a reasonable rate of return, permitting markets to function with less regulation, adopting legislation that deals with how income is to be allocated, allowing host-government participation in the project, and permitting firms to charge a reasonable annual rate for technology and technical services. Several companies pointed to the need for host countries to develop an honest, skilled government bureaucracy and legal system to monitor transfer pricing and prevent its abuse. One extractive firm suggested taxing companies on the basis of physical output rather than profits.

Several transnationals argued that host governments already have sufficient authority to obtain all information necessary to monitor intracorporate transactions. A pharmaceutical company said that the scope for special transfer pricing has been greatly reduced by host-government intervention in recent years and that governments currently dictate the acceptable range of transfer prices. In contrast, governments in developed countries increasingly demonstrate an understanding for firms' needs for special transfer pricing; whereas Third World countries "still have no appreciation of the economic forces that necessitate differential transfer prices." Other transnationals pointed out that a host government can easily discover manipulated transfer prices if the charges are excessive (i.e., over 10 to 20 percent). However, if non-arm's-length transfers take place only on a small scale, the firms regarded the practice as unimportant.

Home countries can also take action. Although many firms claimed that there is little home governments can or should do, several British, German, and American companies noted that their countries already have adequate tax legislation and "tough" tax authorities to deal with any problems. The principle of dealing with subsidiaries on an arm's-length basis was incorporated into the German tax code in 1972. The companies pointed out, however, that their tax authorities are protecting home-country, not host-country, interests. Home countries may also prevent transfer-pricing abuses through legislation barring price discrimination and requiring companies to deal with subsidiaries at arm's length. The Japanese suggested that upon the request of host countries, home governments should investigate abuses and take corrective measures.

Bilateral or multilateral government arrangements to regulate transfer pricing were generally supported by the extractive firms, but the overwhelming majority of manufacturers asserted that such arrangements are unnecessary and/or impossible to administer. A few companies were of the opinion that voluntary guidelines such as those developed by the OECD would be constructive in dealing with special transfer pricing. Those firms that felt that some kind of international agreement might be useful generally concurred that the provisions could not "lump all companies together."

Some companies observed that special transfer pricing raises jurisdictional issues. For example, home-country tax authorities may say that a firm should charge a royalty for technology, but host-country law may prohibit the company from doing so. Within the host country, clashes may occur between customs and income tax authorities. Customs may insist on placing a high value on imported materials or components in order to maximize tariff levies; however, that reduces the company's profits, which, in turn, cuts into the amount of income taxes paid.

With few exceptions, transnationals argued that there is no incentive for firms to minimize their local income by manipulating transfer prices where the home government offers a credit for income taxes paid to the host government and the effective tax rate of the host country is lower than that of the home country. They pointed out that although tax deferral may in theory provide an incentive to shift profits to the host country, in practice other factors are usually more important. For example, many companies said that host-country restrictions on profit repatriation and currency convertibility often act as incentives to minimize local profits. However, several firms did admit to having boosted local profits in order to take advantage of deferral.

An extractive company noted that in its experience, there is an optimal amount of profit to be made in developing countries. If the subsidiary's profits are too high, it is accused of exploitation; if its profits are too low, it is charged with "ripping off" the host country's revenues through transfer pricing. The Japanese maintained that the incentive to maximize profits in host countries is greatest when the host country is also a tax-haven country.

The service-sector companies have generally found that the issue of the manipulation of transfer pricing is only marginally relevant. For example, one retailer said that it ships goods to all foreign subsidiaries at manufacturer's cost, plus shipping and export charges. Banks may occasionally be accused of manipulating their books to take advantage of interest rate differentials in different countries and for different maturities. However, banking officials pointed out that their practices are subject to national regulation and audit and therefore must be "circumspect and correct."

INTEREST AS A
BUSINESS EXPENSE

The Issues

Another problem stemming from intracorporate relations concerns the legitimacy for tax purposes of deductions of interest as a business expense. A number of developing countries have taken the position that when a subsidiary borrows from its parent, the transaction should be regarded as equivalent to an equity investment, and the interest should therefore not be an allowable deduction. Other host countries have proposed the imposition of a withholding tax on interest paid by affiliates to parent companies. Interest can at times absorb a large part of operating income. The question therefore is: How can host countries ensure that intracorporate lending does not become a device for circumventing local corporate income taxes?

The Responses

The interviewed corporations did not regard this issue as particularly critical. Many parent companies, especially the German, French, and British firms, said that they seldom make loans to their subsidiaries. Many British companies encourage their subsidiaries to borrow from local sources. Because the German government has on several occasions treated such interest payments as dividend payouts, German transnationals have been discouraged from lending to their subsidiaries. A U.S. extractive firm claimed that there is actually an incentive for the parent to invest in equity rather than to lend to an affiliate because there is normally a minimum recovery period on loans (e.g., a moratorium on repayment of principal) but no time limit on equity liquidation.

Multinationals that make loans to their subsidiaries said that they do so, not to circumvent local tax requirements, but for other reasons, such as the limited availability of local sources of funds. The firms argued that intracorporate lending, within reasonable debt/equity limits, is a legitimate business practice and should be regarded as such. They saw intracorporate lending as benefiting not only multinationals but also host countries because a smaller burden is placed on local financial resources, freeing them for other investment projects.

The transnationals recognized the potential for abuse in treating interest as a business expense; nevertheless, they generally maintained that developing countries can and do control possible abuses through various rules and regulations. One common regulation is a withholding tax on interest paid by affiliates to parent companies. Although most firms had no objections to this tax, the Japanese were highly critical because they felt it penalizes firms for what is a legitimate business expense. Other host-country regulations cited were limits on the amount of interest that can be paid, requirements that a portion of the funds borrowed from the parent be placed in non-interest-bearing host-government obligations, and legislation making interest nondeductible for tax purposes.

Existing home-country regulations may also help to control possible abuses in the form of excessive interest charges levied by parent companies. In the United States, for example, tax regulations require a parent company to lend to its subsidiaries at an arm's-length rate of interest, which is subject to U.S. tax. In Sweden, the central bank closely monitors all intracorporate lending. Finally, companies noted that subsidiaries are not "puppets" of the parent; if a parent should try to charge more than the market rate of interest, many subsidiaries would seek other, cheaper sources of funds.

Transnationals believed that Third World countries can take further measures to control abuses if they so desire. Companies most frequently mentioned regulations that would place ceilings on debt/equity ratios beyond which debt would be treated as equity for local tax purposes. Another suggestion was that borrowings at maturities exceeding one year should be treated as equity and the returns taxed as income to the parent. An Australian firm proposed that loans be considered equity "to the extent they finance fixed assets and investments." Other suggestions included publication of full corporate accounts with host governments given access to all records and the prohibition of intracorporate loans at interest rates higher than those charged locally.

EXPORT REQUIREMENTS

The Issues

For many countries of the Third World, a major constraint on development is a shortage of foreign exchange with which to pay for required developmental imports. Although some countries are able to draw on past accumulations of official reserves, the current sources of foreign exchange are exports and inflows of public and private capital. Of these, exports are by far the larger, amounting in recent years (for non-oil-producing developing countries) to more than twice the net inflow of capital from all sources.

It is understandable, therefore, that developing countries place major emphasis on expanding their exports and on seeking to harness the operations of multinationals to this goal. The policy of the multinational, on the other hand, may be to produce in the host country strictly for the local market and to supply foreign markets from other affiliates or from the parent company. In some cases, export restrictions may be formally written into patent or technology-licensing agreements by the multinational.

To what extent have transnational corporations had experience with host-country efforts to induce subsidiaries to export locally manufactured goods? Have those efforts come into conflict with company policy? Where such conflict exists, what steps can be taken to reconcile host-country objectives and company policies with respect to exports?

The Responses

Export requirements are a problem primarily for manufacturing companies, many of which believed that the trend toward such requirements is increasing. They reported that developing countries use both formal regulations and informal means of persuasion in attempting to increase their exports. According to one firm, India, for example, may force a multinational to reduce its equity holdings to 40 percent if its subsidiary fails to meet a specified level of exports. Another means used by India and by other countries is to link the granting of import licenses for materials and components to a subsidiary's foreign exchange earnings. Other measures cited by respondents included limits on local sales based on the amount of exports, subsidies and credits, jawboning, and threats of nationalization.

Most manufacturing firms said that they are not opposed to exporting as a matter of policy and that they are sensitive to host-country foreign exchange and balance-of-payments needs. Except for a few companies that do not want their subsidiaries competing in third markets, they said that they would be happy to export from their subsidiaries if it were economically feasible. However, the factual data provided by the companies indicated that except for extractive firms, transnationals generally sell over three-fourths of their local production in the local market.

According to the companies, many host-country requirements are unrealistic in the light of the high costs of local production. Where developing countries induce firms to produce locally by offering a high degree of protection, production facilities are established primarily to serve the protected local market. Because of the high cost of local inputs or diseconomies of scale, locally produced goods are usually too costly to be competitive in international markets. High transportation costs or limited foreign markets for the particular product may also discourage exporting. Nevertheless, Third World countries have imposed export requirements after subsidiaries have been established, leaving the company with the choice of either exporting at a loss or curtailing its operations in the country.

Third-country buyers may be prejudiced against equipment manufactured in developing countries because they believe it to be of substandard quality. One U.S. firm has found that buyers do not want parts labeled "*hecho en Mexico*" even though their quality is the same as the rest of the company's products. Moreover, certain products, such as foods and beverages, do not readily lend themselves to export because they are perishable, too bulky, or tailored to local tastes. Several companies also observed that difficulties are created when neighboring countries try to enforce mutually incompatible export requirements.

German-based corporations cited two additional circumstances that create problems for expanded exports from subsidiaries in developing countries. Many said that as a rule their subsidiaries are fully occupied with expanding supplies of goods to the local market and consequently have little to export. Firms with a high level of exports from the Federal Republic were particularly concerned that increased exports from their Third World subsidiaries could "endanger" home-country exports.

Some companies have had no trouble with host-country export objectives. One U.S. firm said that it finds itself in greater conflict with its local managers than with host governments because the managers are not aggressive enough in seeking new markets. Others have found it difficult to export their usual product lines but have tried to meet host-country export goals by expanding into related nontraditional products for which export markets exist.

India was the country most frequently mentioned as imposing excessive export requirements. A British firm said that it had to sell its goods to the Soviet Union at less than the cost of the raw materials in order to meet an export quota that was a condition for getting a license to import into India. Brazil was also cited as a country that has carried export requirements in particular sectors to extremes. An American company that would like to operate in Brazil regards its export requirements as a barrier to entry.

Exceptional cases aside, the multinationals believed that conflicts with developing countries on this issue can be resolved through compromise. Both parties, they said, should arrive at an agreement before the corporation sets up operations and then should stick to its terms. They believed that host countries must recognize that export expansion is a gradual process; "exports cannot be legislated." Some multinationals suggested that to expand exports, developing countries should increase regional cooperation and form economic unions or common markets with other developing countries.

Other suggestions for host-government action included increasing export incentives and improving the legal and administrative procedures for promoting exports by eliminating red tape. A U.S. firm suggested that developing countries should increase the price of their agricultural exports through cartels or other arrangements so that industrialized countries "pay the price they should" for the products. "Despite their perceptions to the contrary, developing countries will be saved by agricultural exports, not industrial products."

CALVO DOCTRINE AND FORMULA FOR COMPENSATION

The Issues

A number of host governments, especially in Latin America, have written into their foreign investment law the principle known as the *Calvo Clause*, named after the Argentine minister who first propounded it. Under this doctrine, foreign subsidiaries of transnational corporations are expected to give up access to diplomatic support from the home-country government in case of disputes between the foreign investor and the host government and to seek remedies entirely within the local law and juridical system.

The presumption underlying the Calvo Clause is that the authority of the host government would be applied to both local and foreign enterprise on a nondiscriminatory basis. Partly because this presumption of "national treatment" has been questioned, the U.S. government has also sought assurances of "equitable" treatment for its private investors abroad. The principle is particularly relevant to cases of nationalization in which the United States has interpreted equitable treatment as including prompt, adequate, and effective compensation.

To what extent does the Calvo Doctrine act as a deterrent to foreign investment in countries adhering to it? Does the explicit adoption by host countries of national-treatment policies mitigate the effects of the Calvo Doctrine? Can the fear of nationalization be allayed by including in host-government laws specific procedures and formulas for determining the level of compensation?

The Responses

Although many non-American firms had not heard of the Calvo Doctrine by name, most companies reported experiencing host-government objections to subsidiaries' appeals to the home government for support or protection. With few exceptions, however, the doctrine was not regarded as a significant deterrent to private foreign direct investment in developing countries.

Companies said they generally assume that local laws will apply in case of disputes; in fact, they actually prefer this arrangement. Moreover, because host countries are sovereign states, many companies felt that the Calvo Doctrine is reasonable and that subsidiaries should be under host jurisdiction. The doctrine is simply one risk element in making the investment decision and is usually a peripheral consideration. As one U.S. executive noted, "We would never scotch a deal" on the basis of the Calvo Doctrine alone. Companies also pointed out that the doctrine can sometimes be circumvented by agreements providing for neutral third-party arbitration of disputes.

However, some firms did regard the Calvo Doctrine as a strong disincentive to investment. Certain U.S. extractive companies saw it as a "clear signal that the foreign investor will be asked to abandon the diplomatic protection of his home government and the traditional protections of international law." The firm may come under the jurisdiction of a legal system that is not fairly or equitably administered. The problem is compounded, one company asserted, because countries following the doctrine usually display "an aggressive hostility" toward foreign companies. One American manufacturer said that although his company is not directly influenced by the doctrine, other organizations, such as financial institutions, are and that his company might well be influenced by their views.

Most firms said, either explicitly or implicitly, that clear provision for nondiscriminatory national treatment would mitigate whatever disincentive effects the Calvo Doctrine creates. However, German transnationals require that national treatment correspond to minimum international standards. Several firms noted that multinationals often do not receive "fair" treatment in the Third World and that a policy of national treatment would be an improvement over the present situation. One U.S. firm, for example, saw itself as "a widely known symbol of American commercialism" and believed that it is therefore discriminated against when a host government or local group is upset with U.S. government policy. National treatment would, the company felt, help solve this problem.

Other companies questioned whether national treatment would remove the disincentive effects of the Calvo Doctrine. Several Japanese corporations and U.S. extractive firms worried about the ambiguity of the definition of national treatment and were hesitant about surrendering their right to home-country appeal where the substance of national treatment is below the expected international standard or where nondiscrimination is basically given lip service.

On the whole, however, multinationals responding to the question about national treatment agreed that host-government laws cannot allay whatever fears corporations have about nationalization. Although granting that it is the sovereign right of countries to expropriate, few firms would invest in a country if they thought the chances of expropriation were good. Smaller companies believed that because of their size, they are not likely targets for expropriation. Firms that assemble components and high-technology companies did not feel vulnerable to nationalization because the operation depends on a flow of parts or technology from the parent company. Finally, some companies pointed out that "the pendulum of nationalization swings very quickly" in individual countries, so that an expropriated firm may later become reestablished in a country. One bank, for example, reported that it is now moving back into Chile.

In general, the companies believed that their security depends less on specific laws and regulations than on the good will of host governments. If this is present, the need for specific rules is not so great, but if it is lacking, no formula will increase the firms' security.

Multinationals pointed out that any agreement or law relating to compensation could later be repudiated by a government or its successor. Those governments most likely to expropriate without proper compensation are the ones least likely to be concerned with upholding any agreement. The very existence of specific procedures and formulas for compensation provides a certain legitimization for expropriation and causes firms to question the intentions of a host government. Another point, stressed particularly by British, German, and French companies, is that most host-country governments are sophisticated enough to avoid outright expropriation and to use de facto nationalization instead to achieve their goals. Without violating the letter of any local agreement, a government can render an enterprise unprofitable through such measures as raising taxes, forced divestment, price controls, and profit-level restrictions. The result is a "creeping nationalization" against which no agreement could provide full protection.

Determining what constitutes fair and equitable compensation is a major problem. Several companies have had this defined as the net book value of an operation, a procedure that does not compensate a company for lost profit opportunities or investments in intangible assets such as goodwill and marketing efforts. One executive doubted that developing countries would want to change the present system, which calls only for "fair and reasonable compensation," because the ambiguity favors them.

A number of suggestions were made to diminish companies' fears of inadequate compensation in case of nationalization. These included a program, similar to that of the United States Overseas Private Investment Corporation (OPIC), providing insurance based on the original amount of the investment adjusted for retained earnings or accrued interest; the "Indian formula," which, according to one firm, bases compensation on a combination of asset values and profits over the previous ten years; a "multinational fund" to compensate nationalized firms; a formula for compensation under which countries would agree to purchase equity holdings at "so many times their earning capacity"; the submission of compensation disputes to a neutral arbiter, such as the International Court of Justice or a group of international accounting firms; and indexation to adjust the value of invested capital to take inflation into account.

RENEGOTIATION

The Issues

A major strain between transnational enterprises and the governments of developing countries arises from the companies' desire for stability and predictability in their contractual relations and the governments' demands for flexibility. Because investment rests on long-term commitments, firms want reasonable assurance of the terms under which they will operate over the life of the investment. However, host governments may feel that existing arrangements are a vestige of a colonial or neocolonial relationship, that they reflect unequal bargaining power and negotiating skills, or simply that conditions in the host country or in the world market are changing. They therefore often seek the right to reopen the terms of a contract with a foreign business enterprise at any time.

How have multinational corporations reacted to host-country demands for renegotiation, especially in the resource field, where it has been most common? Can the conflicting interests of host governments and transnationals be reconciled by including in agreements provision for renegotiation and specifying the circumstances under which it could take place?

The Responses

The multinationals that addressed themselves to this issue generally showed a flexible attitude toward the question of renegotiation. They were aware of the potential for conflict, but they felt it could be substantially ameliorated if each side displays an understanding of the other's position.

According to most firms, their chief requirement is a stable environment in which to operate, including stability in contractual relations. Instability sours the investment climate. As one firm observed, although conditions in Eastern Europe are "very restrictive," the governments are stable and live up to their agreements. In many Third World countries, on the other hand, the sanctity of contract is ignored. For some companies, stability is so important that they prefer "tough" contracts that are fulfilled to more "favorable" agreements that are subject to frequent changes. For example, stability is particularly vital to firms in the resource field, where the size and long-term nature of investments leave them especially vulnerable to sudden changes in contractual agreements.

Unpredictable changes in agreements not only create problems for existing operations but act as a deterrent to further foreign investment of a long-term nature. For example, one firm said that in some countries, it invests only on the basis of quick returns because "the law changes with the ruler's mind."

Although they oppose arbitrary changes in contractual relationships, multinationals emphasized that mutually acceptable alterations, giving both company and host country time to adjust to new circumstances, can be advantageous to both parties. The conditions under which contracts are negotiated change over time, usually altering the equitableness of any arrangement. Firms were aware that it is difficult for "lopsided agreements" to survive and that host governments do not like to have their freedom of action limited over the long term. "These are the facts of life which any company has to learn to live with," one British company noted.

Host governments are not the only ones who may want to renegotiate contracts; the firms themselves sometimes find that it is in their interest to seek contractual revisions. One extractive company wants flexibility in contracts because it was "stung" when some affiliates negotiated long-term contracts to supply resources to local companies at fixed prices "and then OPEC came along."

Increased communication between multinationals and developing countries is regarded as the best way to reconcile such differences. In addition, several companies proposed that contracts should include clauses allowing periodic renegotiation, perhaps providing for the imposition of penalties if a party reneges on an agreement. However, many French-based corporations felt that such clauses would weaken investment contracts. Some firms believed that conflicts may be minimized through joint ventures in which the multinational holds a minority interest. Also suggested were escape and hardship clauses, which would provide that if conditions change radically, companies may back out of any agreement. One extractive firm said that it provides flexibility through a sliding scale of royalty payments; with each incremental increase in production, the royalty paid to the host country is proportionally higher. Most firms believed that through measures such as these, potential conflicts over renegotiation can be avoided.

However, it should be noted that a small number of transnationals were highly wary of renegotiation. These companies, most of them in the resource field, were concerned that the multinational may be in a disadvantageous position in renegotiation because of the "sheer size and muscle" of the host country and the fact that an investment is not easily reversible. It has been their experience that contractual revisions are not generally conducted on a "rational" basis but tend instead to be highly politicized.

DETERRENTS TO INVESTMENT

The Issues

Two broad types of host-government policies—general policies and policies specifically directed to foreign investment—affect the attractiveness of particular developing countries to foreign investors.

General policies are concerned with the efficiency with which a country uses its domestic and foreign resources in relation to its social and economic goals. Some of the instruments used for this purpose are macroeconomic: monetary, fiscal, and exchange rate policies. Others are microeconomic, affecting various sectors of the economy—for example, tariff policy or sectoral development programs—in different ways. These policies establish the general environment for both foreign and domestic enterprise.

Policies specifically directed to foreign investors include such host-country regulations as local-content requirements, restrictions on access to local finance, export requirements, transfer-pricing limitations, and employment requirements.

Which of these various types of host-government policies are the most serious deterrents to foreign investment?

The Responses

Deterrents to investment in the Third World are matters of degree, not absolutes. Some policies, such as export requirements, are acceptable when pursued in moderation but may be intolerable if pushed to extremes. Moreover, a deterrent is not considered in complete isolation by the firms; rather, it is weighed against the advantages of a project. Resource firms, for example, have to go where the minerals are.

The most important deterrents are instability and the uncertainty resulting from it. Instability exists on at least two levels: sudden and frequent changes in government or in government policy associated with fundamental alterations in the rules of the game under which the parties operate; and the difficulties multinationals have in arriving at clear agreements with developing countries and the day-to-day arbitrariness and inconsistency with which regulations are interpreted and enforced. Many companies pointed out that both types of instability are present to varying degrees in *all* countries, developing and developed.

The transnationals said that if the terms of operation are clear and stable, they can operate in almost any situation, no matter how stringent the regulations, as long as some margin for profit exists. As an example, they pointed to their subsidiaries in Eastern Europe. However, when the whole basis of their operations is subject to unpredictable change, there is no foundation for reliable forward planning. The risks may then become unacceptable, especially for firms that must take a long-run view because of substantial fixed investment. As one U.S. executive observed, "uncertainty is anathema to corporate planning."

Political instability is often associated with economic instability, creating such deterrents as spiraling inflation, unstable currencies, and stagnating markets. However, on the basis of their experience in Chile and Argentina during the 1950s and 1960s, some firms said that they had not found economic instability itself to be an absolute deterrent.

The manner in which rules and regulations are administered in many developing countries is a major deterrent. Excessive red tape, bureaucratic incompetence, indecision, and corruption are common. One firm withdrew from a country because of widespread corruption. Another stated that "things like unkept appointments, unbusinesslike officials, corruption, and inefficiency all put great personal strain on our people. The rewards have to be great to make us persevere rather than do business in places with fewer day-to-day trials."

The companies agreed that these aspects of the general economic environment are more important deterrents than specific host-country policies regulating foreign investment. Of course, most transnationals prefer not to operate under the constraints of host-country regulations such as local-content requirements, foreign exchange controls, divestment requirements, stringent tax laws, restrictions on the use of home-country personnel, export requirements, local financing restrictions, and price controls. Nevertheless, they generally asserted that they can adapt to practically any host requirements as long as the rules of the game are clearly established in advance and adhered to subsequently.

Naturally, in deciding between one developing country and another, transnationals take the extent of host-country constraints into account. Many British and French firms were particularly sensitive to restrictions on remittance of dividends to the home country because the "main goal" of a foreign investment is to earn a profit that can ultimately be distributed as dividends to shareholders of the parent company.

TEN

Home-Country Policies

HOME-COUNTRY INDUCEMENTS TO
INVEST IN THE THIRD WORLD

The Issues

There are three different views concerning the appropriate policies that home governments should follow in relation to private direct investment in the Third World. One view is that an optimum distribution of world resources can best be achieved if the international flow of private capital and other resources is allowed simply to respond to market forces without intervention by public authorities. Hence, the best policy for home governments is one of neutrality, a position that would appear to accord most closely with recent official expressions of U.S. government policy.

The second view is that home governments should actively encourage private direct investment as an element in their general policies of support for growth and development in the Third World. According to this view, home governments should at least try to offset the special risks and disincentives encountered by private investors in the poorer countries because these factors tend to distort the play of market forces.

The third view, which is commonly expressed by trade unionists and their supporters, is that private direct investment should be discouraged because it entails the export of jobs from the home country to low-wage countries.

The issues are what policies the governments of home countries should adopt toward private direct investment in the Third World, what instruments they should use in pursuit of those policies, and how effective such instruments have been in practice.

The Responses

Many transnationals believed that home governments should provide inducements for private direct investment in developing countries. Several stressed the long-term interest of the industrialized world in promoting growth and relieving poverty in the Third World and the role that private foreign investment can play in advancing these goals. One U.S. executive observed, "If we shut our eyes to the increased economic interdependence of the world, we do a disservice to ourselves and the rest of the world. The transnational corporation is the way, within a capitalist structure, for the U.S. to participate [in Third World economic development]."

Some companies also argued that there are short-term benefits to be gained from promoting private direct investment as part of a total foreign aid program. Direct investment can circumvent host-country import barriers and thus help to maintain home-country employment and contribute to a favorable balance of payments, as in the case of assembly and packaging operations in developing countries.

American firms cited another reason: If the government does not actively aid its multinational corporations, they will be at a disadvantage in comparison with other transnationals, particularly the Japanese and Germans. As one manufacturer put it, "We live in a competitive world, and our foreign competitors, especially in other industrial countries, work closely with their governments. We had better wake up to this fact and provide incentives ourselves."

A number of companies opposed an activist policy and favored a neutral stance. Some recognized the definitional problem such a position presents: "Does neutrality mean getting rid of tax credits, deferral, and other appropriate provisions? Or does it mean bringing U.S. firms into a competitive position with . . . other foreign-owned firms?" one manufacturer asked. Companies that favored a neutral home-government policy usually did so provided that neutrality is similarly defined for all parties.

Opposition to an active policy in support of private direct investment was strongest in Britain, where just over half the interviewed firms argued that no inducements should be given. Their primary objection was that inducements could lead to a less than optimal distribution of investment resources by introducing distortions into the market. An American transnational that had previously wanted an activist U.S. government policy no longer supported it. It asserted that if a government encourages private investment, "it assumes a responsibility to defend it." But in practice, the company has found the American government unwilling to do this and therefore feels a neutral U.S. policy is more appropriate.

No company wanted to see private direct investment discouraged by its government, although several American and British firms argued that this is what their governments are in fact doing. In Britain, for example, strict foreign exchange controls "can be an absolute bar" to private direct investment. In the United States, harassment takes such forms as conflicts with the Internal Revenue Service over service fees and the reduction of the nontaxable income limit for U.S. employees overseas.

The tools used by home governments to encourage direct foreign investment vary from country to country. In addition, what constitutes an inducement to investment abroad is subject to differing interpretations. For example, some observers argued that tax deferral promotes foreign investment, but others asserted that it has a minimal impact. Deferral is available to varying degrees in most home countries. With the exception of Italy, home governments also provide different types of investment insurance or guarantees. Sweden makes available both export credit and capital-investment guarantees but limits the latter to developing countries that receive Swedish foreign aid. The U.S. Overseas Private Investment Corporation (OPIC), in addition to offering investment insurance, provides loans and loan guarantees for investment in developing countries. Germany and Japan have adopted more activist policies. Both offer low-interest loans to direct foreign investors. Japan also provides investment loss reserves and equity financing. Germany, through its Developing Countries Tax Law, allows its investors to build up tax-free reserves at the expense of domestic profits for the purpose of investing in the Third World. Through the German Development Company, the German government helps to finance the establishment and expansion of small and medium-sized enterprises in the form of joint ventures.

The transnationals generally said that inducements have not been particularly effective in promoting private direct investment. They considered incentives peripheral in the investment decision, subordinate to such factors as actual or potential market size and host-country restrictions on imports. In addition, incentives frequently only offset some of the disadvantages of operating in developing countries and thus do not constitute an added inducement.

The few companies that have found home-government incentives important were, with the exception of one Australian firm, all American. Tax deferral was most frequently cited as significant in encouraging the reinvestment of earnings, but it is not a substantial inducement for the initial investment decision. The insurance provided by OPIC is mentioned as "crucial" in certain cases. And although the U.S. Domestic International Sales Corporation (DISC) is an export-promotion device, one executive found it important as an investment incentive because developing an export market in a Third World country is usually the first critical step toward the ultimate establishment of local production facilities.

Although most of the respondents found home-government inducements marginal in promoting investment, many felt that they should be continued and even expanded. Few specific suggestions on how home governments can improve their programs were offered, but the consensus was that governments should create a climate both at home and abroad which favors direct investment in developing countries. At a bare minimum, this would mean eliminating the "harassment" many British and American firms felt they had been subjected to by their governments. Several French companies would like to see an end to the double taxation of subsidiaries' earnings.

Other methods of promoting private direct investment were suggested. One possibility is the creation of a closer link between government foreign aid and private investment projects. If, for example, a government helps establish a technical school in a developing country, it should encourage private investment projects to utilize the people trained at the facility. Another proposal is that existing aid programs be reoriented from a country-to-country to a regional basis. For example, to assist Third World countries in meeting their energy needs, help could be provided for the design of regional hydroelectric projects; "normal channels" of private investment would implement the project, but an interest-rate subsidy could be offered as an inducement. A European company suggested that as a part of their foreign aid programs, home-country governments should help to pay the costs of transferring technology; such a policy would do much to overcome host-country reluctance to accept these costs and would thus remove an obstacle to foreign investment.

Should home-country inducements be applied generally or selectively? The companies were evenly divided on this issue. Firms favoring generally applicable inducements pointed to the difficulties of administering selective ones. One U.S. transnational argued that the amount of red tape generated by selectively applicable incentives would make the inducements ineffective. Another asserted that governments could not make "good" choices about when and to whom the inducements would or would not be available. Respondents also attacked selectivity on the grounds that it would run counter to the humanitarian need to reduce poverty in all the countries of the Third World.

Other companies, however, supported selectively applied inducements on the basis of national self-interest. Generally available incentives do not discriminate between friend and foe. If a foreign aid program is viewed as an instrument of a nation's foreign policy, inducements should be used in advancing national goals, whether these include gaining access to mineral reserves or "helping an African country before the Soviet Union does." Selectively applied inducements would also conform to the political realities within each home country, where support could be generated for some projects in certain countries but not for others.

DEFERRAL OF HOME-COUNTRY TAXES

The Issues

In a number of home countries, income tax on subsidiaries' earnings is deferred until the profits are repatriated to the parent company. In terms of the objective of promoting social and economic development in the Third World, this provision has positive effects. It permits host countries to attract foreign direct investment by offering tax rates that are lower than those of the home country. Without deferral, the home country would siphon off any difference between a lower foreign tax rate and its own corporate tax rate. Deferral also encourages the reinvestment of foreign earnings net of host-country tax. Where host-country taxes are lower than those of the home country, deferral in effect converts a portion of such earnings into an interest-free loan to the firm.[1]

[1] The relation between deferral and transfer pricing is discussed in Chapter 9.

To what extent is deferral a feature of home-country taxation? What are the consequences of deferral on the foreign operations of multinationals, particularly in relation to the effects mentioned above?

The Responses

The tax codes of most home countries contain provisions for tax deferral. Transnationals generally argued, however, that it has not been significant in promoting initial investment in developing countries in order to take advantage of tax rates lower than those of the home country. Although low tax rates and deferral could be important at the margin, all incentives are usually secondary considerations in the overall investment decision. Other factors, such as market size, import restrictions, and transportation costs, are far more important. One firm noted it is "an economic truism" that the tax "costs" associated with a given project are only one of several elements taken into account in evaluating its potential return. In addition, host-country tax incentives, whether in the form of low tax rates or tax holidays, are generally considered "illusory" because they can easily be taken away by the host government after a project is established.

One U.S. company disagreed that in the absence of deferral provisions, the home country would siphon off the difference in tax rates. It argued that other factors could mitigate or eliminate any such drain, for example, provisions in the respective tax regulations regarding current expense items; the countries' rates of amortization, depletion, and depreciation of capital items; and the home country's foreign tax credit provisions.

Although most firms attached little importance to deferral and low host-country tax rates for the initial investment decision, there was a sharp difference of opinion between U.S. and non-U.S. firms over deferral's effect on the reinvestment of earnings. American companies typically found deferral of crucial importance in encouraging reinvestment; the others said it is insignificant.

Most American companies believed that deferral benefits both host countries and corporations. Reinvested earnings are extremely important for economic development in Third World countries, constituting one of their principal sources of foreign capital. The elimination of deferral would be "a body blow" to developing countries because "reinvested capital would go out the window." Deferral is significant to

American multinationals because it increases the pool of investment resources at their disposal. If it were eliminated, foreign earnings of U.S. companies would be taxed when earned rather than when realized as dividends. Without deferral, the companies said, they could not effectively compete with other multinationals, such as those based in Germany and Japan.

Several U.S. companies agreed that where host-country taxes are lower than home-country taxes, a portion of reinvested earnings is, in effect, an interest-free loan to the firm. However, others objected to this view. One executive pointed out that although host-country tax rates may be lower, any difference may be recouped later by the host government through withholding taxes on dividends paid to the parent firm. Another asserted that "whereas a loan is an agreed amount which is intended to be repaid, deferral represents a decision by the government not to exact a contribution to the public treasury." A third firm said that because the American government does "nothing" to protect multinationals' interests abroad, the profit earned there "does not belong to the U.S. government. . . . Suppose they could tax our foreign earnings, and we get nationalized. Would the government share the losses as well as the profits?"

Most non-U.S.-based transnationals and a few American companies stated that deferral has not increased their reinvestment of local earnings. For corporations based in Britain and Sweden, this may be due to direct home-government pressure. One British firm said that the Bank of England has "leaned on us" to repatriate profits as soon as possible. A Swedish firm reported that it had to agree to repatriate its profits when earned in order to receive government permission to send capital abroad. Other corporations noted that some tax agreements partially offset the effects of deferral. Several companies pointed out that as long as profitable investment opportunities exist in a country, investment will occur with or without deferral. If, however, these opportunities have been exhausted, deferral could encourage a misallocation of resources by providing an inducement for reinvestment.

One U.S. transnational maintained that deferral does not promote reinvestment because there are forces that counterbalance its incentive effect. For example, although deferral makes additional funds available for reinvestment, the resulting increased exposure to potential foreign exchange losses argues for repatriation of profits as soon as possible.

INVESTMENT INSURANCE

The Issues

Some home governments provide various forms of insurance to transnational enterprises to facilitate a flow of capital and other resources to the developing countries. The United States, for example, offers insurance against the risks of currency inconvertibility, war, and expropriation.

The question of insurance raises a number of issues: How effective is such insurance as an inducement to foreign investment? Should the insurance be offered generally for investment in Third World nations or only selectively for investment in those poorer countries unable to attract private foreign capital on their own? Should the insurer avoid inherently unstable wholly owned equity investments in natural resources in favor of joint ventures with local interests or perhaps management contracts? Should the insurance be multilateralized to the maximum extent and include financial participation by developing countries to reflect a mutual stake in encouraging foreign investment in the service of development?

The Responses

The transnationals expressed a wide range of views about the significance of investment insurance. As in the case of other inducements, however, the availability of insurance is only one factor among many considered before an investment is made and in most cases is not a major consideration.

Investment insurance, which may take the form of export-financing guarantees or capital-investment guarantees, is generally available in most home countries. Sweden, however, offers export credit guarantees but does not have a practical system of capital-investment guarantees. Swedish firms were of the opinion that insurance is an important inducement to investment where it is available and believed they are at a competitive disadvantage because of the lack of workable capital-investment guarantees in their country.

Because insurance helps to limit investment risk, most companies saw its availability as an additional factor in favor of a given investment. According to one U.S. firm, lack of insurance coverage for a given country serves as a "red flag." It is unlikely, however, that the absence of insurance would automatically eliminate an investment project.

Most American transnationals have found that the insurance offered through OPIC is too limited in its coverage and too expensive for high-risk areas. One asserted that insurance was probably more important in the past, when corporations were relatively inexperienced in dealing with the Third World. Other firms, both American and non-American, said that the risks where they invest are too small to make insurance a significant inducement. The French have found their system "ponderous" and difficult to use. Japanese companies claimed that because their insurance has been denominated in dollars, its effectiveness is reduced when the yen appreciates against the dollar.

In the opinion of most firms, investment insurance should be generally applicable and available and should not discriminate against any group of Third World nations. Some transnationals favored lower insurance rates for the poorest countries. However, one stated that the prime function of insurance is to offset risk and that reductions in investment risk are at best "loosely correlated" with increases in host-country wealth.

Furthermore, companies generally did not want insurance restricted to particular types of investments. Several disputed the assertion that wholly owned equity investments in resource ventures are "inherently unstable," arguing that all types of investments should be encouraged as much as possible. One pointed out that it may be in the home country's interest to promote natural resource projects by offering insurance because this helps it to secure needed raw materials.

In contrast, some firms argued for more selectivity in investment insurance in order to permit the insurer to minimize risk or to further the home country's foreign policy goals. Selectivity could be based on the type of investment or limited to capital risk in physical assets. No firm proposed limiting insurance to those countries unable to attract private direct investment on their own. An Australian company suggested a two-tiered insurance program that would favor joint ventures and management contracts over wholly owned resource ventures but would not eliminate insurance for the latter.

Most transnationals also favored some type of multilateral investment insurance and the financial participation of developing countries in such a program; however, few believed that either is a real possibility. The companies would support multilateral insurance if it means government-backed political-risk insurance offered collectively by industrial nations through international insurance agencies because it might make more insurance funds available and thus promote investment in developing countries. It could eliminate the competitive advantage of those firms that at present have access to insurance over those that do not. Multilateral insurance might also "spread the risks," reduce costs for the insurers, and improve the benefits to those using insurance. Many French firms were in favor of action by the European Communities to establish a communities-wide insurance program or to harmonize national systems.

Most of the corporations supported financial participation by developing countries in any program because joint action would increase trust among the parties and would demonstrate that the countries do have an interest in encouraging private direct investment.

Companies generally had doubts about the feasibility of multilateralized insurance because of potential organizational problems. Several believed there would be disputes over terminology and the size of members' contributions. In addition, differences among countries would, according to one executive, require "case-by-case" treatment. Companies also doubted whether developing countries have the financial resources to participate in such joint action. However, it was thought that higher-income Third World nations could contribute to the scheme.

A small number of transnationals opposed multilateral insurance, arguing that national insurance schemes are more efficient and practical. One U.S. company saw multilateral insurance as a "backdoor financing mechanism" open to abuse. Another argument offered was that if insurance becomes widely available, it would encourage a host-country attitude of "Well, it's insured. Let's nationalize."

EXTENSION OF HOME-COUNTRY
JURISDICTION TO FOREIGN AFFILIATES

The Issues

Foreign affiliates are established under the laws and jurisdiction of the host countries in which they operate. At times, however, home countries attempt to extend their own laws and regulations to the foreign affiliates. This practice may place the affiliates at a competitive disadvantage with respect to firms not subject to such extraterritoriality. It can also create jurisdictional conflicts between home and host countries in which the company is caught in the middle. As a consequence, tensions have been created in such fields as antitrust, capital-flow controls, restrictions on trade with Communist countries, and more recently, efforts to prevent corrupt practices in host countries.

The basic questions raised here are: What experiences have multinationals had with such attempts to extend home-country jurisdiction? What limits should be set on the jurisdictional reach of domestic law as it affects the operations of subsidiaries abroad?

The Responses

U.S. and non-U.S. firms were clearly divided over the extent of home-country attempts to extend jurisdiction over foreign affiliates. Most non-U.S. firms have experienced few such attempts except for several cases of requirements for repatriation of earnings. The policies of the European Communities and the United Nations with respect to southern Africa have affected several German transnationals.

On the other hand, almost all American transnationals and even some non-U.S. firms have encountered U.S. government efforts to extend its jurisdiction to overseas subsidiaries. Antitrust regulations were most frequently cited; many U.S. companies asserted that they are at a competitive disadvantage because of "overextended" U.S. antitrust legislation. "We hamstring ourselves in terms of our ability to do business abroad," complained one executive. A non-U.S. company became entangled in U.S. antitrust investigations because of its relationships with subsidiaries of U.S. firms. According to an American executive, the problem may be the result of the different approaches of U.S. and European antitrust legislation. U.S. law stresses protection of the competitor, whereas European law emphasizes the protection of the user/consumer. The American government has also extended its jurisdiction in such areas as corrupt practices, the Arab boycott of firms doing business with Israel, trade with Communist countries, and capital controls.

In general, the transnationals wanted the jurisdictional reach of the home government kept within its borders. However, they acknowledged certain specific exceptions: when an illegal overseas action has a substantial impact on the home economy; when parties to a contract agree in advance that home-country laws will apply, as in the case of dispute settlement; and when national security is threatened.

Most corporations that have been affected by the extraterritorial application of home-country law said that although they do not like this practice, they can usually live with it. An extension of home jurisdiction creates two different types of problems: The first, which companies have been able to adapt to more easily, results from projections of home-country jurisdiction that place the multinational at a competitive disadvantage by limiting its freedom of action. The second, which respondents said was more difficult to adjust to, results from home-country policies that run directly counter to host-country legislation and goals, regardless of whether the firm is placed at a disadvantage compared with other companies. For example, an American company observed that it is only reasonable for the Mexican government, in line with its general policy of stimulating exports, to encourage a U.S.-owned subsidiary to trade with Cuba, even though such trade is prohibited under the U.S. Trading with the Enemy Act. Several companies also noted that the extension of home-country jurisdiction, by infringing on the host country's sovereignty, may sour the investment climate for all multinationals.

CORRUPT PRACTICES

The Issues

Pressure to engage in corrupt practices such as the bribery of local officials can arise either from host-country government officials or from within the firm itself. Where host governments play a large role in economic affairs through direct controls and regulation, opportunities abound for putting pressure on firms either for the private gain of particular officials or to bolster the position of a political party. Similarly, companies may engage in corrupt practices either to influence political events or to gain preferential economic treatment.

The issues are the extent and nature of such practices and how they can best be dealt with.

The Responses

Many transnationals were troubled by the phrase *corrupt practices*. As one executive put it, "Like the word *sin*, it is susceptible to rather broad interpretation." For example, the practice of a business making contributions to a political organization is accepted in some countries, frowned upon in others, and illegal in still others.

Companies divided the kinds of pressures they receive and the actions they may take as a result into two groups: legitimate and illegitimate. Legitimate pressures include subtle demands or formal requests to do things that a firm would not normally do but that are not patently illegal or unethical. A British corporation, for example, was encouraged to "arrange things so as to ensure that there were substantial and visible benefits for local inhabitants" in order to "counter secessionist tendencies." Such urgings are tolerable up to a point, and companies generally feel a need to try to accommodate governments within reason. Illegitimate pressure includes the solicitation of money or jobs for a political party or faction or for individual host-country nationals. Companies are much more likely to refuse to accede to this type of request.

Because of the ill-defined boundary between acceptable and corrupt practices, it is difficult to judge how extensive the latter are. No company admitted that it has bribed or attempted to bribe host-country officials or that it has been illegally involved in the politics of a host country. On the other hand, about half said that they have experienced some type of pressure, either legitimate or illegitimate, from host-government officials. With one exception, however, the French corporations stated they have not faced such requests. Several firms pointed out that pressures from governments occur frequently in the industrialized world as well as in developing countries.

Companies with little experience in this area tended to hold that firms should "refuse to bow" to illegitimate demands. Firms accustomed to such requests were usually more flexible in their responses, arguing that it is sometimes more "prudent" to comply. For example, one transnational explained that "you have to learn to live with [the pressures]," and another suggested that the requests "should be steered into modest and understandable limits." However, none of the firms said it automatically yields to any demands made on it.

Many of the firms said that if the pressure is serious enough, they would withdraw from the country and that they have refused to invest where improper demands seem likely. Ethical questions aside, several of the companies said it would be shortsighted to yield to such requests; transnationals undertake long-term investments, and any improper support for the party or officials currently in power would be likely to alienate those who may come to power in the future.

Although the respondents were divided about what should be done to counter these pressures, they were generally united in asserting that regulating corrupt practices is not the job of the home country except in such "blatant" cases as ITT in Chile and the Lockheed scandal. Home-country legislation is likely to prove unwarranted and ineffective; it could even prevent companies or their officers and employees from exercising legitimate political rights. Insofar as corruption occurs in host countries, it is *host*-government action that is critical. Moreover, home-country interference is patronizing because it attempts to export the industrialized world's standards of business morality to the developing world. If the host country wants to end corruption, it can do so, as is demonstrated by the example of Singapore, where anticorruption measures are vigorously carried out.

A small number of firms supported home-country efforts to control corruption abroad. Some favored home legislation that would recognize the differences among countries and their customs. Others would encourage all home attempts to limit corrupt practices.

About half of the firms saw disclosure as one alternative means of controlling corrupt practices, though not necessarily an effective means. Disclosure would help keep companies "within the confines of what can stand public scrutiny." It might also help them to resist pressure for illegal payments and increase host-country awareness of what is and is not accepted practice in home countries. A British firm favored a disclosure requirement like Belgium's, under which payments are openly disclosed and firms engaging in improper practices are subject to severe tax penalties. The skepticism expressed by some transnationals about disclosure's effectiveness centered on enforcement difficulties.

Several corporations opposed disclosure. The Japanese were particularly hostile to it. One "strongly questioned" the use of disclosure to reveal actions that are legal in some countries but not in the country seeking the information. Others opposed disclosure because the requirements may go too far or overburden the companies. It may be difficult, for example, to distinguish between legal agents' fees and illegal bribes.

Most transnationals agreed that they can and should voluntarily take steps to limit corrupt practices. There was strong support for company codes of conduct and internal monitoring to control illegal payments abroad. Many said that they already have codes that include flat provisions against bribery and political involvement in the host country, with severe penalties for employees who violate the rules. Through these codes of conduct, companies hope that they can keep corrupt practices to a minimum and avoid raising corruption to new levels or introducing it to countries where it does not exist.

Support was also widespread for international efforts to deal with the problem through voluntary codes of conduct, such as the OECD guidelines and the International Chamber of Commerce's efforts toward self-regulation. Several firms pointed out that international codes accepted by both foreign and domestic enterprise would help eliminate the disadvantages under which some companies operate.

HOME-COUNTRY ROLE IN DISPUTES

The Issues

The broad questions are what role home governments should play in issues arising between host governments and transnational enterprises and whether home governments should intervene to ensure fair treatment for their companies.

More specifically, if a host country expropriates foreign property without prompt, adequate, and effective compensation, should the home government intervene? If so, should it resort to such punitive measures as suspension of foreign aid to the expropriating country, negative votes on loans being considered by multinational development banks, and denial of trade preferences? How effective are such measures likely to be?

The Responses

The dominant opinion expressed by the interviewed corporations is that home governments should play a minimal role in most issues arising between transnational enterprises and host governments. At most, home governments should provide general support on broad policy issues, such as encouraging host-country governments to give fair treatment to foreign investment.

Home governments should use available diplomatic channels, including the negotiation of bilateral treaties on issues such as investment guarantees and double taxation. More direct intervention, such as bringing pressure to bear on international lending agencies to tie credits to a host country's conduct toward foreign investors, would be ineffective, inappropriate, and counterproductive. Several companies felt that by resorting to home-government pressure, multinationals "may win the battle and lose the war." As one manufacturer stated, "You can't club the countries to effect change."

Some felt that action taken by the corporations themselves can solve particular problems. In one case, a company persuaded other firms not to invest in a particular Third World country until the company was compensated for expropriated property; the country ultimately gave in.

Despite the limited role they envisaged for their home governments, the companies reported that they generally maintain some contact with home-country embassies. However, they expressed a wide range of views on the importance of such contacts. Some transnationals from each home country found them highly useful, particularly for exchanging information and coordinating embassy and subsidiary activities so that the two do not work at cross-purposes. One corporation has found that businessmen tend to undervalue the work of their embassies because the results are seldom immediately demonstrable. Other firms noted that although close contact with home-country embassies is valuable, the transnational's own contacts within the host country may be more important. For example, several banks said that if an issue arises, they get together and go as a group directly to the central banking authority, rather than work through home-country embassies.

Many British and American corporations reported that although they maintain communication with their embassies, they have usually found such contact to be of limited usefulness because embassy personnel do not support the firm and are not well informed about business. One transnational, for example, said it was forced by the Indian government to sell 60 percent of its equity; when it asked its embassy for advice, the reply was "you're on your own." The companies asserted that, with some exceptions, commercial attachés do not know their jobs. One American official argued that embassy personnel, not the companies, should take the initiative in keeping close contact between the two groups "because the companies probably have better access to information and policy than the embassy."

Several firms believed that subsidiaries should have little or no contact with home-country embassies. They maintained that such contacts hinder the integration of the subsidiary into the local community.

In the case of serious disputes between transnationals and host countries, such as uncompensated expropriation, firms said they usually call for home-government intervention and support. Except for the French and most Swedish companies, the firms that responded to the question generally favored some type of punitive action by the home government, arguing that "expropriation without compensation is theft; it is criminal." Among the punitive measures they suggested are denial of trade preferences, negative votes on loans being considered by international development banks, and expropriation of the host country's property in the transnational's home country. No corporation proposed that home governments intervene militarily to protect their investments. "The days when the government could run the gunboats up the Zambezi River are over."

Although some transnationals believed that punitive actions should be taken regardless of the circumstances, many noted that home-government response should depend on the particular case. An American executive argued that if the host action is against foreign enterprise in general, the U.S. government should counteract with all appropriate means. If, however, expropriation is aimed at a single company, a more cautious approach is called for because the host government's action may be justified.

In contrast, several firms said they believe that the home government should not take punitive measures. A harsh home-government response might anger the host government, jeopardizing the position of all foreign investment in the country.

Although many transnationals advocated punitive home-government action, few were convinced that it would be effective in solving or mitigating serious disputes. Only two firms unequivocally asserted that such action would be effective. Swedish multinationals invariably said that Sweden, because of its size, cannot affect the outcome of most disputes.

The willingness of home governments to adopt punitive measures was questioned by many multinationals on the grounds that relations between host and home governments involve many elements in addition to the issue in dispute. Japanese companies doubted the effectiveness of home-government measures as long as other nations are willing to help the country being penalized. This feeling was echoed by an American executive, who stated that home governments may be able to accomplish little unless they act together. Several officials observed that the leverage of a home government varies directly with the host country's dependence on its aid. As foreign aid and trade become increasingly multilateralized, the leverage of any single home country will be diminished.

POLITICAL CONSIDERATIONS IN FOREIGN INVESTMENT

The Issues

Company investment policy may be affected not only by the economic conditions and prospects in host countries but also by the social and political situation. How do the firms react to serious violations of human rights and other objectionable conditions that may prevail in particular developing countries? Are investment decisions in such cases guided by public opinion, personal judgment, or home-country legislation or regulations? Where home-country restraints do not now exist, should they be adopted?

The Responses

There was a high degree of unanimity among multinationals on this issue. Almost invariably, firms said that the political situation in a country affects their investment decisions. In many cases, companies have refrained from investing or reinvesting in particular countries because of unstable political conditions.

Risk assessment, rather than more abstract concerns, is a key consideration. As one firm explained, "Ethical and moral considerations should not enter into the investment decision. Business considerations should dominate." Either implicitly or explicitly, companies observed that there is a clear difference between a political *system* and a political *situation*. The fact that a firm disapproves of a given regime or its policies generally does not prevent it from investing in or trading with the country if the commercial prospects appear favorable. A bank executive observed that "we cannot be the world's correctional officers." Angola, Mozambique, and several Eastern European countries were cited as examples of countries in which firms do business despite their dislike for the existing system.

Some companies stated that it is difficult to evaluate moral considerations. For example, how is the term *human rights* defined? "Was the dictatorship in South Korea a violation of human rights or a measure of self-preservation in the face of a very real North Korean threat?" one firm asked. Others pointed out that most nations could be faulted on some aspect of their political life.

Several transnationals said that they hope that by working within the political systems in countries whose policies they may deplore, they can improve the living conditions of both their own workers and the general population. An American firm operating in South Africa stated that "our investment creates jobs. We have been encouraged by certain black African countries not to disinvest there."

If, however, the political situation in a country poses risks to the long-term viability of a project—for example, through the likelihood of civil war, invasion, or government overthrow—firms will be extremely reluctant to invest. South Africa was most frequently mentioned as the country in which political instability threatens investment.

With the exception of cases in which legislation prohibits trade with, or investment in, specific countries, investment decisions are based primarily on the personal judgments of the firm's chief executive and board members. They take many factors, including risk, potential profitability, and stockholder reaction, into account. In certain cases, public opinion is important. Several companies have curtailed or abandoned projects because of the fear of a public backlash both at home and in important third-country markets.

Although it is regarded as inevitable that considerations of political risk affect investment decisions, only one company believed that home-government regulation is desirable or can be effective in this area. However, several firms felt that some intervention may be justified in particular cases involving national security. An Australian firm observed that regulations tend to take on a life of their own, persisting long after the reason for their introduction has ceased to exist.

ELEVEN

International Programs and Arrangements

ALTERNATIVE CHANNELS FOR FINANCIAL TRANSFERS

The Issues

Three proposals for increasing the flow of private capital to developing countries have been put forward by the United States at recent international meetings: the creation of an international investment trust to mobilize portfolio capital for investment in the Third World, an increase in the capital of the World Bank's International Finance Corporation, and the creation of an International Resources Bank to guarantee foreign private loan capital invested in extractive projects in developing countries.

One set of issues is whether the companies favor these or other initiatives for mobilizing foreign private capital for developing countries outside the traditional framework of private equity investments and how effective they believe such initiatives might be.

A related issue is the access of developing countries to the national capital markets of the developed countries. Bond markets in particular are subject to a variety of constraints such as foreign exchange regulations in Europe and legal restrictions imposed by states on institutional investors in the United States. What can be done to widen the access of private firms and public entities in developing countries to the bond markets of the industrial countries? Should some sort of international guarantee mechanism be established?

The Responses

The transnationals expressed qualified support for proposals designed to increase the flow of private portfolio capital to the countries of the Third World on a multilateral basis. Some favored such initiatives because they could promote the development of infrastructure or other host-country projects not readily undertaken by private enterprise. Other firms noted that official aid is likely to fall short of the needs of developing countries and that increased private-sector investment will have to help "fill in the gap."

Such support, however, was subject to reservations. Several companies were of the opinion that portfolio capital should supplement, but not replace, the traditional framework of equity investment through the transnational enterprise. Moreover, as one company said, "the problems of developing countries cannot be eradicated with massive capital flows." Obstacles to Third World economic development lie not only in a shortage of financing but also in, for example, a lack of technology and of managerial and marketing skills. One firm noted that although low-cost credit has a role to play in development, steadily increasing debt cannot solve host-country problems because debt servicing, even at low interest rates, can become a serious drain on foreign exchange earnings.

Some transnationals opposed any new initiatives for mobilizing foreign private capital. Several argued that if a developing country has "a good track record," it can raise any money it needs in existing private markets. Another concern voiced by some respondents was that the proposals could lead to an unbundling of the investment package. A Swedish company believed that the proposals "imply undue centralization of capital flow," which might be disadvantageous to individual developing countries.

Extractive firms in general were particularly critical of the proposal for the creation of the International Resources Bank, calling it "total nonsense" and a "nonstarter." They maintained that the bank could not be negotiated practically to assist private projects only; less efficient public projects would also have to be included.

There was some disagreement about how effective the proposed measures would be. Some transnationals believed that the initiatives, particularly those involving World Bank participation, would encourage additional private capital flows to developing countries, but more were of the opinion that the initiatives would have only limited effectiveness. One executive observed that the past record of government-supported efforts has not been good. Japanese corporations doubted that the measures would be endorsed by many countries. Other restraining factors cited were the inability of developing countries to mobilize the appropriate technological and managerial resources to support the investment and the problem of determining how the investment risk would be shared.

The Adela Investment Co., S.A., a private group formed by transnationals and banks from Western Europe, Canada, Japan, and the United States, was highly recommended as a model by a number of respondents. The chief objective of Adela is to support small business enterprises in developing countries by making minority investments in them. According to the corporations, Adela has proven "quite successful" in Latin America, and similar initiatives should be undertaken in other regions of the developing world.

On the related issue of increasing access to international bond markets, Japanese corporations suggested that as a precondition, developing countries should make public all necessary financial and economic information. Other firms called for liberalized profit-remittance regulations. Industrialized countries could offer fiscal incentives for investments in bonds floated by developing countries, require domestic financial institutions to accept such bonds in a given proportion to the size of the domestic captial market, and relax annual quotas on bond issues. One official argued that collective guarantees would have to be provided so that debt repayments "will not subsequently dry up . . . at the whim of spendthrift governments."

Approximately half of the companies believed that developing countries already have sufficient access to international financial markets and that these are flexible enough to meet the specific needs of any borrower. The availability of private credit, however, has encouraged some Third World nations to overborrow, causing a curtailment in their freedom to use international bond markets. Although favoring the free access of developing countries to these markets, the firms maintained that the ultimate criterion for full acceptance is a country's creditworthiness. "Lenders can't be forced to put their money into high-risk areas against their will."

Because of this problem, many companies felt that an international guarantee mechanism is needed if the developing countries are to make full use of international financial markets. One firm suggested that the industrialized countries and the members of OPEC jointly establish such a facility. There was some doubt, however, about its practicability.

GUIDELINES FOR THE ACTIVITIES OF MULTINATIONALS

The Issues

A set of guidelines relating to international enterprises has been adopted by the member governments of the OECD. Similarly, an effort is now under way in the United Nations to establish a code of conduct applicable to the operations of multinational corporations in developing countries.

The issues are whether the transnationals support the current U.N. effort; how they believe their governments should react to the demands of the developing countries that the U.N. code should be mandatory rather than voluntary and applicable to multinational enterprises but not to domestic enterprises or to governments; and whether any code negotiated in the United Nations should be supplemented by voluntary codes adopted by multinationals themselves, either singly or in concert.

The Responses

With the exception of French companies, the multinationals generally expressed halfhearted support for U.N. efforts to establish guidelines for their activities. Swedish and Australian manufacturing firms not engaged in high-technology activities were most receptive to the U.N. proposals, believing that they are the best way to achieve consensus on acceptable norms of behavior.

Most companies had no objections to the U.N. initiative as long as it is not "one-sided." The "balanced" approach taken by the OECD (which includes obligations for both companies and governments) was seen as the most constructive way in which the United Nations could proceed. Some British, German, and American manufacturers expressed only grudging acceptance of the U.N. action: "It is not something we can be against." The adoption of the codes was regarded by several as inevitable. "You have to learn to swim with the tides," observed a British official.

Doubts were commonly expressed about the impartiality of the United Nations. One official charged that the world forum treats the multinational issue as a *political* rather than an *economic* problem. "The U.N. action is rooted in political rhetoric designed to force changes in the basic *control* of multinational operations in host countries." Another called the negotiators "incompetents who use invalid criteria."

Because of these opinions, several firms opposed the U.N. initiative, calling it a "holy war" directed against the transnationals. In general, French corporations were particularly vehement in their opposition to the codes of conduct, finding them "unrealistic, inefficient, and useless." One firm called such codes "a cheap way to buy a false good conscience." Another believed that by attempting to regulate company conduct, the codes would add another distortion to international trade.

Other multinationals were against any internationally negotiated code because there is already excessive government interference. An American executive believed that any problems are best handled through host-government regulation. "The governments should be free to establish whatever conditions they deem desirable for multinational operations. The multinationals, however, should be free to determine whether the situation is attractive enough to warrant any investment."

If a code is to be accepted, its underlying principles would have to be essentially those of the OECD guidelines: nondiscrimination between foreign and domestic and between public and private enterprise, provisions for national treatment, and inclusion of responsibilities of governments as well as companies. The Japanese stated that any guidelines should be minimal and should apply to all enterprises, both foreign and domestic. A Swedish manufacturing firm was the only corporation to argue that the codes should apply to multinationals only. "The world is still in a highly unequal situation. . . . To create more equality under such circumstances, it seems quite appropriate to have rules pertaining only to the strong parties." Most enterprises also wanted a code to be voluntary rather than mandatory. An American company pointed out that if the code followed the OECD principles, it would be respected even as a voluntary document. Another found the distinction between mandatory and voluntary guidelines artificial; "the key issue is to develop a system of joint values between the involved parties." However, several Swedish firms favored a mandatory code.

Many transnationals stated that if a code does not follow these principles, it will be the developing countries that will suffer because they will lose foreign investment. In order to ensure that U.N. guidelines observe the OECD principles, the active participation of the OECD countries in the U.N. negotiations was supported by many firms. A U.S. extractive company stated that "the OECD countries should not 'cooperate' with the U.N. effort; they should attempt to mold it." The Japanese believed that it is "safer" for multinationals to arrive at a mutually negotiated code rather than to have host countries act unilaterally. French firms, however, generally said that they do not want to be associated with the formulation of the codes.

No matter who participates in the negotiations over a code or what principles are used in designing it, the companies were largely skeptical about the possibility of agreement being reached. Because of the existing diversity of views and circumstances, any code would probably involve "sweeping generalities" or "overwhelming specifics." As a British firm observed, "any code is a long way down the road."

Some officials, especially Americans, did advocate voluntary action by multinationals in the form of company codes of conduct. An Australian manufacturer endorsed concerted action by the firms through the International Chamber of Commerce to set up a code of conduct.

INTERNATIONAL HARMONIZATION OF TAXES
AND TARIFFS

The Issues

Tax concessions and tariff protection are among the most important inducements employed by developing countries to attract foreign investment. The use of these devices may have adverse effects on development, however, for two reasons: The costs incurred may not be justified from the standpoint of rational use of the host country's own resources, and the incentives may lead to expensive competition among developing countries for foreign investment, the effect of which is to alter artificially the country destination of investment without necessarily increasing its total volume.

The issue is whether these problems can be mitigated through some degree of international harmonization of national policies that affect the taxation of transnational enterprises and their protection from foreign competition.

The Responses

Transnationals expressed the same skepticism about multilateral efforts to harmonize national tax policies and protective trade measures that they showed on the issue of an international code of corporate conduct. "All of these ideas about harmonization are great in theory, but they are not practical," one firm said. The diverse economic and political interests in the developing world make these initiatives "utopian ideas." Countries cannot and should not be expected to surrender much of their sovereignty over the conduct of economic policy. A developing country requires flexibility in the choice and use of tools to achieve its social, economic, and political goals.

Moreover, companies said it is not necessarily true that harmonization would benefit all developing countries. Uniformity of tax policies without uniformity in other investment incentives could favor investment in those countries able to offer the highest level of nontax incentives, encouraging them to compete in nontax inducements to investment. Tax harmonization could also hurt developing countries that are dependent on tax incentives to attract foreign investment. Similarly, harmonization of protective trade measures could make it difficult for some countries to encourage both foreign-owned and locally-owned domestic production.

Nevertheless, the companies generally were not opposed to all efforts to harmonize tax policies and protective trade measures. Many enterprises, particularly U.S. manufacturing firms, asserted that although it may not be possible or desirable for *host* countries to harmonize their tax policies, benefits could be derived from home-country harmonization of taxes. They saw a commonality of interest among the industrialized countries that makes such action feasible. Harmonization would eliminate some of the "artificial" competitive distortions experienced by firms of different home countries when operating abroad.

Similarly, although full harmonization among developing countries may be impossible, those countries with common characteristics may form regional groupings, such as the Latin American Free Trade Association (LAFTA), in which coordination of tax policies may occur. As an alternative, bilateral tax treaties can be, and have been, used to deal with some of the jurisdictional conflicts arising between countries. A Swedish firm believed that a "general international code recommending how to approach the problem of tax incentives" might be useful. An American executive suggested that a code be negotiated giving developing countries special exceptions so that they could use incentives to attract capital; these incentives could be phased out over time.

By and large, transnationals said that they do not believe it necessary or desirable to place limits on tax incentives for foreign investors in any tax agreement. Again, restrictions would constrain the host country's freedom of action. An American extractive firm felt that to preclude foreign investors from taking advantage of tax incentives while making them available to domestic investors puts the foreign entrepreneur at a disadvantage. Japanese companies stated that tax incentives are necessary to compensate for the increased risk of operating in the Third World. Three American companies did favor limits on these inducements; indeed, one proposed that tax incentives be entirely prohibited.

Harmonization of protective trade measures encountered stronger opposition and, according to some firms, would be more difficult to achieve than tax harmonization. Several companies feared the consequences of agreements in the trade area. Where tariffs have been used to induce local production, harmonization could cause problems for enterprises that depend on a tariff wall for protection from import competition. In other cases, such as that of textiles, tariffs have been used to subsidize failing domestic industries. Japanese transnationals, although favoring limited coordination in this area, preferred the continuation of present policies because policy changes have usually caused losses for the firms. According to some executives, opposition to harmonization of protective trade measures would also be likely from local producers dependent on protection. As one official noted, trade barriers have a local constituency, but tax incentives for foreign-owned firms do not.

Another problem is that in cases in which trade barriers have been used to offset overvalued exchange rates, countries would have to take action in the monetary field to compensate for the effects of harmonization. Several American corporations suggested that the countries end overvaluation, either through floating exchange rates or a downward-crawling peg. The Japanese proposed that countries strengthen their currencies by more effectively mobilizing private savings so that domestic interest rates decline and investment rises, thus spurring economic growth.

Because of these difficulties, most firms stated that it would be a waste of time and effort to try to harmonize protective trade measures on an international level. Some believed, however, that bilateral or regional arrangements, such as the Central American Common Market and the

European Economic Community, may be a practical and useful way of harmonizing trade policy for the participating countries and of creating a larger internal market for the group as a whole.

INTERNATIONAL ANTITRUST CODE

The Issues

Concerns have been raised about transnational firms' restrictive business practices such as export limitations, price collusion, market allocation, and the abuse of industrial property rights. On the recommendation of the Group of Eminent Persons appointed by the United Nations to study the role of transnational corporations in the development process, work is going forward on an international antitrust code. The question is how the companies react to this approach to the problem of restrictive business practices.

The Responses

Most firms addressing the issue view the possibility of an international antitrust code with a high degree of skepticism. While few had strong objections, almost all believed that such a code would be impossible to achieve.

The corporations recognized that a code might help simplify the multiplicity of local laws and practices in this field, but they argued that it would be extremely difficult to reconcile existing national differences. The best that could be agreed upon would be a general outline of vague principles that would not be worth the time and effort necessary to reach agreement. One company doubted that even a watered-down code could be negotiated because important countries, such as Japan, support restrictive business practices.

Even if agreement could be reached, there would be problems of interpretation and enforcement. An American firm pointed out that "in the United States, where there is over eighty years' experience in interpreting [antitrust] legislation, what these laws mean is still a subject of great controversy." On the issue of a mandatory versus a voluntary code, the companies were divided. Some would not oppose a mandatory code if it covered both public and private enterprise and if it was based on the principle of national treatment. Others wanted only a voluntary code identifying areas of mutual concern for business enterprises and governments.

Several firms were against including provisions on export restrictions and market allocation on the grounds that they would harm both transnationals and developing countries. One official argued that "if transnationals can't allocate markets and restrict the exports of their subsidiaries, then they will generally have to operate in the lowest-cost locations, which in most cases are not developing countries." Another stated that these practices help achieve an orderly flow of goods and services. Otherwise, fluctuating demand could cause "long cycles of depressed commodity prices" that are generally harmful to host-country economic development. More generally, a code that would apply to arrangements among affiliates of a transnational was considered particularly objectionable.

Other firms, although not opposed in principle to an international antitrust code, did not support U.N.-sponsored efforts in this area, which they believed reflect an animosity toward transnationals and do not show "an understanding and acceptance of the desirability of competition as an economic way of life."

The companies proposed some alternatives to an international antitrust code. Several felt that strengthening national legislation would be sufficient to control restrictive business practices. Some said that existing legislation could be supplemented through voluntary guidelines like those developed by the OECD. Other suggestions included regional antitrust codes and an international antitrust "advisory body."

INTERNATIONAL CENTRE FOR THE SETTLEMENT OF INVESTMENT DISPUTES

The Issues

The World Bank's International Centre for the Settlement of Investment Disputes (ICSID) provides machinery for conciliation and arbitration. Its work thus far has been very limited, however, mainly because of the nonparticipation of many countries, especially in Latin America, on the grounds that disputes in their countries should be settled under national jurisdiction. This raises the issues of whether and how to widen the use of ICSID or other international fact-finding and arbitral procedures in disputes between host governments and multinational enterprises.

The Responses

Most transnationals supported international dispute-settlement mechanisms and offered a variety of proposals for increasing their use. One British firm, noting the sensitivity of host countries to perceived threats to their sovereignty, suggested having arbitration machinery associated with groups such as the Association of Southeast Asian Nations (ASEAN) or the Andean Pact. In this way, "there may be more chance of their [the host countries'] accepting arbitration . . . under the auspices of regional organizations of which they are members and which are independent of the main industrial countries." Many extractive firms believed that the way to widen the use of ICSID or similar mechanisms is to negotiate investment agreements that include international arbitration. One extractive company reported that it includes in its concession agreements a provision for a third-party arbitrator whose decision is final. In reaching that decision, host-country law is applied.

The Japanese, as well as a few other firms, suggested a number of "tie-ins" among international bodies to widen the use of international fact-finding and arbitral procedures. These would include the compulsory use of ICSID by World Bank loan recipients or preferential lending by the World Bank to cooperating countries and the negotiation of bilateral investment treaties between host and home governments that would include dispute-settlement provisions.

Other ideas mentioned were reinforcing the conciliation and arbitration function of the International Chamber of Commerce and the International Court of Justice, establishing a set of rules or a code on international investment dispute settlement, and including the conciliation and arbitration procedures used by ICSID in agreements between multinationals and host governments.

A few companies felt that in time the use of international conciliation and arbitration mechanisms will become more acceptable. "So long as some host countries insist on being judge, jury, and law enforcer simultaneously, there is nothing that can be done except to wait for a change in attitude." One Australian corporation felt that it is a question of trust and of understanding Western legal principles; "the more it [ICSID] is used, the more it will be used."

Part III

Summary and Conclusions

TWELVE

Summary and Conclusions

Over the last several decades, an extensive literature has been spawned on the role of transnational enterprises in the Third World, most of it highly critical. In recent years, the disquiet has increased as the demands of the developing countries for a "new international economic order" have intensified. In response to those demands, the United Nations is currently sponsoring several major international negotiations designed to "tame the multinationals" by establishing codes of conduct to regulate their behavior in general and in the more specialized fields of the transfer of technology and restrictive business practices.

Despite the concerns expressed by developing countries, the flow of private direct investment from the industrial nations has been increasing. As a proportion of the total flow of external capital to the Third World, however, private foreign direct investment has remained fairly constant. Just under half the stock of this investment is of U.S. origin, and almost 45 percent of the total is located in Latin America. Although petroleum and manufacturing each account for about a third of the foreign direct investment, the share of manufacturing is on a pronounced upward trend.

The interview results presented in Part II are not intended as "facts" about the impact of transnational corporations on the development process in the Third World. Rather, they are to be regarded as a set of attitudes and perceptions about host-country concerns expressed by individuals who have had major and extensive responsibilities for the operations of multinationals in developing countries. Many of the individuals interviewed had not previously been familiar with the full range of host-country concerns except in the most general way and had never before been in a position in which they had to ponder these issues and react in explicit terms.

TOWARD MUTUAL UNDERSTANDING AND PRAGMATISM

Much of the past debate on this subject has been a dialogue of the deaf. The multinationals have traditionally proclaimed "good corporate citizenship" as their guiding policy, calling attention to their substantial contributions to the Third World in such terms as the number of workers they employ, the volume of local taxes they pay, and the stimulus they provide to economic growth and industrialization. The developing countries have, on the other hand, charged the multinationals with a long list of sins of commission and omission, including stifling local entrepreneurship, using excessively capital-intensive processes, and failing to respond to such national goals as promoting income redistribution and greater regional balance within the countries.

What we have observed, therefore, is a discourse on two levels. The transnationals focus on the performance of the firm, where efficient and profitable operation is deemed automatically to bring benefits to all: directly to those who relate to the firm through the purchase and sale of goods and services, including labor, and indirectly to the rest of society through the payment of taxes. The critics, however, go beyond the internal calculus of the corporations and stress the perceived broad social, political, and economic consequences of the existence of subsidiaries of powerful foreign enterprises in the midst of poor countries struggling to achieve not only economic growth but also greater economic and political independence and social equity.

One of the interesting findings of the survey is the basic sympathy among the multinationals for the broadly stated national goals of the developing countries. Many of those interviewed may disagree with the critical assessment of the consequences of the companies' operations. They generally do not, however, question the legitimacy of host countries evaluating the impact of the multinationals on the developing countries in terms of the latter's own broad national goals.

It is apparent from the interviews that an important evolution has taken place in the attitudes of transnationals toward the growth process in the developing countries and toward their relationship to that process. To a much greater extent than in the fifties and sixties, the corporations recognize both the diversity of circumstances in the Third World and their own need for flexibility in their approach to individual countries. There is also less of a tendency to regard the historical process of transformation now taking place in much of the Third World as a replica of the industrialization process that occurred in the now-developed countries during the eighteenth and nineteenth centuries. As latecomers to development, the nations of the Third World are in a profoundly different position, and many are confronted with problems of poverty and population pressure on a scale that exceeds anything experienced by the Western world during the period of its industrialization.

With this new perspective on the development process has come a greater willingness on the part of many multinational corporations to accept some of the constraints imposed on their activities and mode of operation in the countries of the Third World. Moreover, they have discovered that the consequences for the firm have rarely been catastrophic and in some instances have indeed been beneficial. In any case, the flame in a number of burning issues in relations between multinationals and host countries has substantially gone out as the corporations, regardless of home country, have accepted many aspects of the host-country position, sometimes in their own interest and sometimes because they had no alternative.

A few examples of accommodation may suffice at this point. With few exceptions, multinationals employ and train host-country nationals for their foreign operations not only for unskilled and skilled manual jobs but for all levels, including technical, financial, and managerial positions. In many instances, the managing director of the foreign affiliate is a local national. Company self-interest and national policies of indigenization of employment happen to coincide nicely in this field. The multinationals' attitude toward joint ventures has also changed. Although company opinion was divided, a substantial majority of firms is willing to accept some local equity participation. "We have fewer hangups on this subject today," said an executive of one firm whose historical position had been to insist on 100 percent ownership. A further example is the prevailing attitude toward the Calvo Doctrine, under which foreign subsidiaries are required to give up access to diplomatic support from their home governments in cases of dispute and to seek remedies entirely within the local law and judicial system. The Calvo Doctrine may be an additional risk element, but the firms generally accept the legitimacy of host-country insistence on the supremacy of local law and, with the exception of extractive companies, do not regard the doctrine as a significant deterrent to foreign investment.

Just as transnationals have been increasingly accommodating to the changing realities in the Third World, a significant evolution has been taking place in the attitudes of governments of developing countries. Longer contact and experience with multinationals have given host-country governments a better understanding of how the corporations operate and an appreciation that the relationship need not be of the zero-sum variety but can be one of mutual gain. In many developing countries, stronger economies and better-trained individuals have led to greater competence and confidence in dealing with the multinationals and a growing tendency to take a pragmatic approach to the relationship.

These impressions of a growing host-country pragmatism are derived from the actual experiences of multinationals in negotiating and dealing with Third World governments. By no means do these perceptions apply to all developing countries. Where they do not apply, however, the chances are that not much foreign investment is taking place. Moreover, the impressions are based on the reality of contact with officials on a practical level in host countries, not on the rhetoric of their political representatives in the United Nations and other international forums. In the view of many officers of transnational enterprises, that rhetoric presents a quite distorted picture of the current state of thinking about multinationals in the principal host countries of the developing world.

It would be a mistake, however, to convey the impression that a convergence of views has developed between multinationals and developing countries on most of the issues that concern host governments. Substantial differences of perception persist, and they exacerbate whatever conflicts and tensions are inherent in the relationship.

Nor should it be assumed that there is anything monolithic about the attitudes of the multinationals. This summary attempts to capture the dominant view, but a wide spectrum of company opinions exists on most issues, as the detailed discussion of the interview responses in Part II clearly demonstrates. Moreover, the views of particular multinationals generally depend heavily on the industrial sector in which their affiliates operate and only to a minor extent on the nationality of the parent firm.

THE INTERVIEW RESULTS

Effects on Local Entrepreneurs

One set of host-country concerns relates to the parts of the economy in which a multinational establishes its affiliates. To the extent that the multinationals enter fields in which local firms already exist or where the near-term potential for local enterprise is significant, the fear exists that incipient indigenous entrepreneurship will be stifled. To the developing countries, this threat is enhanced by the tremendous technological and financial advantages of the multinationals as well as by their advertising, promotion, and product-differentiating practices.

In the extractive and high-technology manufacturing sectors, such local competition as is encountered is usually from other foreign enterprises rather than from indigenous firms. Active competition from local firms is not uncommon, however, in such manufacturing fields as food processing, textiles, and other consumer sectors. Nevertheless, the charge of smothering was regarded by the multinationals as invalid. In fact, they believed that their presence actually stimulates local entrepreneurship through the upgrading of local products, expanded markets, and backward and forward linkages with the domestic economy. In any case, local firms are often given special dispensations and considerations by their governments to offset the alleged advantages of foreign companies.

Import Substitution

Developing countries also express concern about the establishment of subsidiaries in domestic industrial sectors that are protected from foreign competition in order to encourage industrialization. As a consequence, they claim, the stimulus to industrialization often fails to benefit indigenous enterprise, while the local economy bears the cost in the form of implicitly subsidized higher prices and possible excessive profits accruing to foreigners.

Most foreign manufacturing firms conceded that their investment decisions are heavily influenced by host-country policies of sheltering domestic markets. Given the choice, the companies would prefer to export from their home base rather than produce locally. Once subsidiaries are established locally, however, protection for a considerable period is often essential to their survival and continued profitability because of the high cost of domestic production.

The firms rejected the idea that the local economy is disadvantaged when their subsidiaries operate behind the shelter of tariffs and other protective devices. Regardless of whether foreign or domestic firms enjoy protected markets, real costs are incurred for the host country in the form of higher prices for locally produced goods than those that prevail for comparable goods on the world market. There are, however, trade-offs for these costs: the potential benefits in the form of the boost to industrialization and possible foreign exchange savings. Additional benefits brought by foreign firms are increased access to capital and technology and the upgrading of technical and managerial skills. Moreover, host governments can, over time, reduce the costs and increase the benefits of import substitution through measures such as local-content requirements and through gradually phasing out protection and exposing the sheltered industries to international competition.

Entrepreneurial Initiative

Third World representatives complain that local subsidiaries are afforded little scope by parent companies for entrepreneurial initiative and that foreign affiliates are therefore more in the nature of extensions of the parent firm than an integral part of the local economy. The interviews confirmed that projects involving major capital expenditures require parent-company approval. With respect to other initiatives, however, the degree of entrepreneurial freedom given to subsidiaries depends on the sector in which they operate. Tightest central control appears to be exercised by extractive and high-technology corporations. In other fields, subsidiaries are given substantial freedom to diversify into related products.

Unbundling

Unbundling of the foreign investment package is seen by many developing countries as a means of gaining domestic control of important sectors of the economy and increasing the net returns to the host country from the use of foreign resources. Few transnational enterprises welcomed unbundling, and their responses to such pressures varied. The willingness to accommodate to this pattern of resource transfer is greatest in the extractive field and least in high-technology manufacturing. Host-country leverage to induce unbundling is strongest in the extractive field both because of the location of the resources in the host country and because of the transnational's heavy initial capital investment, which becomes hostage to the host government. In high-technology manufacturing, however, the bargaining power of the firm is greater because of the dependence of the local operation on a continuing flow of technology over which the parent firm may exercise quasi-monopolistic control.

The respondents expressed a wide range of opinion on the prevalence among Third World countries of the desire to unbundle, except in the natural resource field, where unbundling is already the pattern. On one aspect of this issue, however, virtually all firms agreed: The cost to the developing country of this method of acquiring financial, technical, managerial, and marketing resources from abroad is substantially greater than the cost of the standard foreign investment package.

Local Borrowing

Concern is voiced in developing countries about the extent to which multinationals borrow locally rather than commit their own financial resources to their subsidiaries. Apart from not adding sufficiently to the capital stock of the country, this practice is alleged to deprive local projects of their only source of financing. The multinationals acknowledged that they raise capital from local sources, explaining the practice mainly in terms of the desire to minimize foreign exchange risks. But most companies denied that they deprive domestic firms of finance and noted that host countries often severely limit the access of foreign firms to local borrowing. Moreover, profit repatriation limits may be related to a company's equity investment. Where profits are not repatriated to the home country, whether by choice or because of host-government regulations, they may be invested short term within the host country and thus add to local financial resources. However, the extent to which these additions to local resources offset the totality of local borrowing by multinationals is an issue that cannot be resolved on the basis of the responses of individual firms.

Conflicting National and Corporate Goals

The dichotomy between national and corporate goals is often stressed by Third World critics of transnationals. Corporate goals, which are determined by parent companies, may relate to such matters as profit maximization, diversification of raw material supplies, preempting or maintaining a foreign market position, or achieving some overall rate of growth in sales and earnings. National goals, on the other hand, are of a different order. They may include employment maximization, export stimulation, maximization of tax revenues, rural development, and other broad social and economic objectives.

Companies acknowledged that conflicts may arise because of the disparity between the two sets of goals, but they believed that the problem has little to do with the foreign nationality of the parent company. Rather, it is a consequence of the difference between public and private aims. In fact, the policies of foreign firms were claimed to be more socially responsible and to serve host countries' national objectives better in many cases than those of domestic enterprises.

Takeovers

Developing countries tend to frown on foreign investment in the form of the acquisition of going local businesses, regarding such takeovers as alienating the domestic economy without providing offsetting benefits. For reasons of their own, not many multinationals displayed enthusiasm for acquisition as a method of entering a developing country either. When they do take over a local business, however, they rarely do so to continue operations as before. New products and techniques may be introduced, new markets may be developed, and the entire operation is likely to be made more efficient. Nevertheless, as the respondents pointed out, if developing countries find takeovers objectionable in principle, they possess the means to prevent or control such acquisitions.

Technology Transfer: Adaptation of Products and Processes

A major aspect of the relationship between host countries and multinationals about which host-country complaints have been most insistent is the transfer of technology. Three categories of concern have been especially prominent: the appropriateness of the technology, the terms on which it is transferred, and the need to develop an indigenous R and D capability.

The question of appropriateness relates to both products and processes. Products manufactured by local affiliates of multinationals are often said to be too sophisticated, too highly designed, and too well packaged to meet the needs of masses of low-income people. Instead, they cater to the consumption demands of the elite. Even more important is the appropriateness of the productive processes, particularly whether they are excessively capital-intensive in relation to the abundance of cheap labor in the host countries. If they are, the employment problem is intensified, inequalities of income are aggravated, and the balance of payments is worsened by excessive importation of capital equipment.

According to the transnationals, product adaptation does take place, necessitated in some cases by host-country regulations requiring the use of local materials and components. The willingness of firms voluntarily to adapt their products, however, is constrained by various factors, including the small size of many local markets, the insistence of customers on the latest and most advanced products, and the need for worldwide product uniformity to maintain quality (as in the case of pharmaceuticals) or to provide for the interchangeability of parts (as in the case of transport and agricultural equipment).

Adaptation of processes to local conditions is common in the manufacturing sector, but particular adaptations are less extensive among high-technology firms than among other manufacturers. The reason foreign firms do not appear to take full advantage of the abundance of cheap labor in Third World countries is that, paradoxically, labor-intensive processes may in practice be less economical. Skilled labor is often scarce in developing countries, and capital-intensive processes frequently require less skill than more labor-intensive methods do. The advantages of cheap labor may be offset by the costs of designing a new process, training and supervising large numbers of local workers in an unfamiliar setting, and ensuring the quality, uniformity, and dependability of the output of labor-intensive processes. Other reasons cited by the respondents included host-country restrictions on the import of used equipment and on the laying off of workers when demand for the product declines.

On the whole, transnationals attached little weight to more general host-country policies that are widely cited in the economic literature as biasing company decisions toward more capital-intensive methods. Such policies include overvalued exchange rates that reduce the cost of imported machinery, tax concessions based on the amount of invested capital, and low or negative real rates of interest. It is unclear, however, to what extent the small importance given to these subsidies reflects the absence of explicit treatment of them in the company's internal accounting.

Licensing of Technology

Licensing is regarded by many developing countries as a highly desirable way of acquiring foreign technology without the loss of domestic control over an enterprise inherent in the traditional direct investment relationship. Their principal concerns about this method of purchasing technology, whether patented or unpatented, are the allegedly excessive prices charged and the restrictive conditions often attached to the licensing agreements. Among the most objectionable of the latter are clauses requiring the licensee to purchase materials, components, or equipment from the licensor; limitations of sales to the domestic market or to designated foreign markets; and "grant-back" provisions conveying to the licensor all rights to improvements.

The companies rejected the argument that royalties paid for technology are excessive because the expenses incurred in developing it have already been sunk. They believed this attitude is based on a misperception of technology as a stock rather than as a flow. When viewed in the latter sense, it becomes apparent that payments for technology must be sufficient to maintain the flow of innovation on which economic progress ultimately depends.

Companies that include restrictive clauses in licensing agreements justified them on various grounds. Tie-in clauses to materials and components from the licensor are explained as quality-control devices needed to protect the trademark or brand name. Export restrictions in licensing agreements are intended to prevent competition among different licensees of the same company. In this respect, American corporations claimed to be at a disadvantage in comparison with other multinationals because U.S. antitrust legislation, applied extraterritorially, prohibits most attempts by American firms to include export restrictions in licensing agreements with nonaffiliated companies, although transactions between related companies are usually not affected. More generally, licensing agreements are increasingly subject to screening by host-country governments that insist on the elimination of restrictive export provisions.

Research and Development

Because foreign technology is often regarded as inappropriate, high priced, and subject to restrictive conditions, Third World countries have sought to reduce their dependence on imports of technology by encouraging the development of an indigenous R and D capability. The reaction of multinationals to this issue was almost uniformly negative; they cited the lack of an adequate pool of qualified people, the economies of scale in research and development, and the inadequate market size of most developing countries. Many of their subsidiaries do, however, have facilities for quality control, product testing and adaptation, and technical trouble-shooting; and these operations have the potential, in some countries, to evolve into an indigenous R and D capability.

Linkages

A common host-country complaint is that certain types of foreign operations partake of an enclave character in the sense that they have few backward linkages (i.e., the purchase of local inputs) or forward linkages (i.e., the domestic use of the firm's output in further productive operations) with the domestic economy.

Host governments have attempted to encourage closer integration of foreign operations with the local economy in various ways. One method is local-content requirements for foreign manufacturing operations. With few exceptions, the companies have not found these to pose serious problems. Another method of achieving backward linkages is through subcontracting, a practice widely followed by most firms in their own interest. Even in the extractive field, subcontracting takes place, but largely in construction, transport, and other ancillary services. Mandatory forward linkages, however, are a problem for the extractive companies because further local processing of raw materials involves heavy capital outlays and is often uneconomical.

Host-Country Incentives

Incentives of various kinds are granted by developing countries to encourage industrial development generally and to attract foreign investment specifically. Tax holidays and other fiscal incentives are the most common type. Although welcoming and taking advantage of such concessions, very few of the firms believed them to be crucial to the investment decision. If a subsidiary is unprofitable, which is often the case in its early years, it will not be able to take advantage of tax holidays and other common forms of tax concessions. Far more important are the "fundamentals" affecting the profitability of an operation, such as market size and growth potential.

Transfer Pricing

Transfer pricing is an issue about which the developing countries have expressed great concern. A substantial proportion of the transactions of foreign subsidiaries in some industries are intracorporate purchases and sales. It is alleged that the transfer prices on such transactions often diverge from arm's-length prices because of attempts to exploit, to the benefit of the company and to the detriment of the host country, differences in economic policies in the various countries in which the transnational corporation operates. The relevant policies may include income taxes, import duties, repatriation limitations, and price controls.

For most firms, however, manipulative transfer pricing is said to be contrary to company policy. Only a few isolated firms said they use special transfer prices, and none of them regarded its resort to this practice as a means of avoiding the payment of host-country taxes. They said it is used only to cope with restrictions on the payment of royalties and fees for technology, limitations on charging administrative expenses to foreign affiliates, price controls on final products, and restrictions on the repatriation of earnings.

If unreasonable restrictions of this kind were removed, the inducement to manipulate transfer prices would be substantially eliminated. Other suggested steps for host countries to take included auditing invoices obtainable from subsidiaries and comparing them with world market data to determine fair value. An extractive firm suggested taxing companies on the basis of the physical volume of output rather than on profits.

Interest as a Business Expense

Another problem arising from intracorporate relations is the legitimacy for tax purposes of the deduction of interest on intracorporate loans as a business expense. Because interest can at times absorb a large part of operating income, intracorporate lending can become a device for circumventing local corporate income taxes. A number of developing countries have therefore taken the position that when a subsidiary borrows from its parent, the transaction should be regarded as equivalent to an equity investment and therefore not deductible.

Multinationals that lend to their subsidiaries said they do so, not to circumvent taxes, but for other reasons, such as the limited availability of local sources of funds. Within reasonable debt/equity limits, intracorporate lending was regarded by the companies as a legitimate business practice. Various methods were mentioned, however, for controlling abuses, such as ceilings on debt/equity ratios beyond which debt would be treated as equity for local tax purposes, imposition of withholding taxes on interest paid by affiliates to parent firms, limits on the rate of interest payable to parents, legislation making interest nondeductible for tax purposes, and treatment of borrowings at maturities exceeding one year as equity, the returns on which would be taxed as income to the parent.

Increasing Exports

Developing countries place major emphasis on increasing their exports in order to pay for their expanding requirements of developmental imports. To this goal, they have naturally sought to harness the operations of local affiliates of multinationals through both formal regulations and informal means of persuasion. They claim, however, that foreign manufacturing firms resist their export-expansion efforts because company strategy favors producing in host countries strictly for the local market and supplying foreign markets from the parent firm or from affiliates in other industrial countries.

Most manufacturing firms said that they are sensitive to host-country balance-of-payments problems and foreign exchange needs and that they would be happy to export from their local subsidiaries if it were economically feasible to do so. The main problem, however, is that host-country industrialization strategies based on import substitution typically result in high costs for local production behind the shelter of steep tariffs and other import restrictions. Unless offsetting export subsidies are granted or corrective exchange rate action is taken, the locally produced goods cannot compete in world markets. Other deterrents to exporting are the prejudice of some foreign buyers against equipment manufactured in developing countries and the fact that certain products, such as processed foods and beverages, do not readily lend themselves to export because they are perishable, too bulky, or tailored to local tastes. Despite these problems, companies do try to meet host-country export goals, some even going so far as to expand into unrelated products for which export markets exist.

Stability versus Flexibility in Contractual Relations

A major source of strain between multinationals and host governments arises from the desire of the companies for stability and predictability in their contractual relations, on the one hand, and the demands of the governments for flexibility, on the other. Because investment rests on long-term commitments, firms want reasonable assurance of the terms under which they will operate over the life of the investment. Host governments may feel, however, that existing arrangements reflect an earlier condition of unequal bargaining power and negotiating skills or simply that conditions in the host country or in the world market have changed. They therefore often seek the right to reopen the terms of a contract with a foreign business enterprise at any time.

Although they opposed arbitrary alterations in contractual relationships, multinationals recognized that conditions change over time and that "lopsided agreements" are unlikely to survive. Moreover, it is not only host governments that may want to renegotiate contracts; the firms themselves may also find it in their interest to initiate revisions. Flexibility to renegotiate alterations is therefore potentially advantageous to both parties and can be provided through carefully drawn escape clauses or provisions allowing periodic renegotiation.

Corporate Social Responsibility

Social responsibility is a term often used by multinationals in characterizing their approach to doing business in developing countries. Generally, the term comprehends the strict observance of local laws; adherence to high standards of business ethics in dealing with suppliers, customers, and workers; and support of community activities in such fields as health, welfare, education, and cultural affairs. Although some companies have gone so far as to formalize their approach to social responsibility in a code of corporate behavior, most simply assert their adherence to such guiding principles of corporate conduct.

But standards of corporate social responsibility in this sense fall considerably short of meeting the broad social and economic goals of developing countries, such as greater local control of their own economies, employment creation, export promotion, income redistribution, indigenization of technological adaptation and change, and rectification of the regional imbalances and economic duality that are so common in countries undergoing rapid structural transformation. To advance these goals, governments of developing countries intervene in the market through taxation, inducements, regulation, and negotiation, all of which are designed to bring private business behavior more directly in line with their public goals.

By and large, the multinationals understand and accept this role for the governments of developing countries. What they mainly seek is a clear articulation of national goals and a reasonably stable framework of law and regulation that can be taken into account in their investment decisions and in their subsequent business operations. In addition, some Japanese firms suggested that methods be devised to measure transnationals' social contributions to host-country objectives.

Role of Home-Country Governments

Insofar as home governments are concerned, there is general agreement that although their role should be limited, it should be one of encouraging private direct investment because of the long-term interest of the industrialized countries in relieving poverty and promoting growth in the Third World. As one U.S. executive observed: "If we shut our eyes to the increased economic interdependence of the world, we do a disservice to ourselves and the rest of the world. The multinational corporation is the way, within a capitalist structure, for the United States to participate [in Third World economic development]." Another reason cited by American firms for U.S. government support is that without it, the companies would be at a competitive disadvantage compared with other multinationals that do receive encouragement and incentives from their home governments.

A dissenting view is that an optimum distribution of world economic activity can best be achieved if the international flow of private capital and other resources is allowed simply to respond to market forces without intervention by public authorities. Hence, the best policy for home governments is one of neutrality, a position corresponding most closely to recent official expressions of U.S. government policy. The main support for this view, however, came, not from the American firms, but from the British.

No company supported a third view of the role of home governments: namely, that private direct investment abroad should be discouraged. This position is commonly taken by American trade unionists, who see foreign investment as depriving the home country of needed capital and causing the export of jobs to low-wage countries. Several U.S. and British firms complained, however, that their governments do, in practice, discourage foreign direct investment through such policies as exchange controls on capital transactions (in the case of the United Kingdom) and conflicts with the tax authorities over service fees and the exclusion limit for overseas employees (in the case of the United States).

Although most multinationals favored home-government encouragement of direct investment in developing countries, the range of incentives currently offered is quite limited. Tax deferral is granted in most of the countries that participated in this study, but in none is it specific to developing countries. Investment insurance is also common. Japan and Germany appear to offer the most extensive set of inducements, including low-interest loans by government financial institutions, equity financing (in the case of Japan), and the right to accumulate tax-free reserves (in the case of Germany).

Like host-government incentives, inducements granted by home governments were generally regarded as secondary considerations in the original decision to invest in developing countries. There was a sharp difference of opinion, however, between U.S. and non-U.S. firms concerning the effect of tax deferral on the reinvestment of earnings. American firms generally found deferral to be of crucial importance in encouraging reinvestment; whereas others regarded it as insignificant.

Investment Insurance

Unlike deferral, the importance attached to investment insurance was greater among firms based outside the United States. Here again, however, the availability of the incentive is, in the majority of cases, an additional factor favoring an investment, not a major consideration. Most firms favored some type of multilateral insurance as a means of spreading the risks and reducing the costs. They would also welcome the financial participation of developing countries in such a program as a means of increasing mutual trust among the parties and demonstrating host-country interest in encouraging private direct investment. But strong doubts were held about the practical possibilities of establishing a multilateral program.

Jurisdictional Conflicts

Conflicts of jurisdiction between home and host governments have been experienced by a majority of U.S. firms and by some non-U.S. firms, but few regarded the problem as really serious. By and large, the companies believed there should be greater limits on the jurisdictional reach of home governments as it affects subsidiaries abroad. Antitrust regulation is the principal area of contention for U.S. firms, who alleged that it has placed them at a disadvantage in comparison with foreign competitors. Other home-country regulations that have involved jurisdictional conflicts include capital controls, politically motivated trade restrictions, antiboycott legislation, and transfer pricing. In the latter case, home-country tax authorities may, for example, insist that companies charge a royalty for technology, and host-country law may forbid it.

Corrupt Practices

There has been an increasing effort, particularly in the United States, to regulate corrupt practices abroad. These practices may be initiated either by host-government officials or by the firm itself. No clear consensus emerged concerning what can be done to control corrupt practices. A strong current of opinion, however, is that home countries should not attempt to export their own standards of morality to the rest of the world and that the problem is primarily one of host-country legislation and enforcement. Although financial disclosure requirements by home governments were regarded by some companies as a useful regulatory mechanism, most believed them to be ineffective and to intrude needlessly into sensitive financial areas. Company codes of conduct, however, were seen as an important means of controlling corrupt practices.

Home-Country Role in Disputes

The majority of companies in all sectors believed that home governments should play a minimal role in issues arising between host governments and multinationals. Most firms, however, maintain some contact with home-country embassies. But many British and American firms and some others said that they find these contacts to be of little value. Only in the case of a serious dispute, relating, for example, to compensation for expropriation, would any of the firms want the home government to intervene. A considerable spread of opinion existed, however, on how effective home governments can be in such cases and on whether punitive measures, such as the suspension of foreign aid or the denial of trade preferences, can be useful deterrents to arbitrary host-country action.

Objectionable Social and Political Conditions in Host Countries

Repression and other objectionable social and political conditions in a foreign country naturally affect multinationals' investment decisions. The key consideration from the company perspective is, however, not abstract principles but the extent to which unstable conditions affect business risk and performance. Companies must also take stockholder reaction and public opinion into consideration. A number of firms stated that in countries where serious violations of basic human rights exist, they believe that they can help to alleviate conditions by working within the system. With one exception, companies did not see a need for more home-government regulation in this field.

International Agreements

As for international arrangements to mitigate Third World concerns about the operations of multinationals, most firms favored only a limited role. Those responding to the question would generally support some suggested multilateral initiatives for increasing the flow of foreign private capital to developing countries outside the traditional framework for corporate equity investment, such as enlarging the resources of the World Bank's International Finance Corporation and the creation of an international investment trust to mobilize portfolio capital for local enterprises in the Third World. The firms were also generally receptive to a coordinated effort to remove legal and administrative constraints on the access of developing countries to private bond markets while emphasizing that even with freer access, the creditworthiness of the borrower is ultimately the deciding factor.

Support was lukewarm at best for U.N. efforts to establish a code of conduct for transnationals because many firms distrust the United Nations in this field. Whatever support existed was generally predicated on the OECD guidelines for transnational enterprises serving as a model for a U.N. code, that is, on its being essentially nondiscriminatory between foreign and domestic enterprise, on its including obligations on the part of governments (including state enterprises) as well as private enterprises, and on its being voluntary rather than mandatory. A general skepticism about the value of a worldwide code pervaded the responses, however, because conditions vary in different countries and such a document would inevitably reflect the lowest common denominator of a wide spectrum of signatory views. It would be likely, therefore, to contain mostly sweeping generalities.

Similar skepticism was expressed regarding the desirability or feasibility of proposals for international harmonization in the antitrust and tax fields. Any effort to include in an antitrust code constraints applicable to intracorporate transactions would be particularly objectionable.

Whatever merits international tax harmonization among developing countries might have in theory, it was regarded as simply not practical. Developing countries have conflicting interests that lead some to provide greater tax incentives for foreign investment than others do. In any case, nations are unlikely to surrender an essential part of their sovereignty.

Dispute Settlement

Dispute settlement is the area in which widest support for international action exists among the multinationals. The suggestions for strengthening the international role included reinforcing the conciliation and arbitration functions of the International Chamber of Commerce and the International Court of Justice, establishing an international code on the settlement of investment disputes, including the conciliation and arbitration procedures of the World Bank's International Centre for the Settlement of Investment Disputes in agreements between transnationals and host governments, and making the use of the Centre by recipients of World Bank loans compulsory.

Apart from dispute settlement, the role favored for international bodies in relations between multinationals and developing countries is extremely limited. Nor do the companies see their home governments playing much more than a supportive, though generally nonactivist, role except in major crises.

In the final analysis, the companies believed that the main prospect for enhancing their contribution to the development of the Third World lies in building on the greater sense of mutual interest that is already beginning to evolve directly between themselves and host countries. Transnationals, on the one hand, must increasingly recognize that most Third World governments are committed to the goal of fulfilling the social and economic needs of their people. They must accept the fact that this often requires modifications of private business behavior through constraints as well as inducements. Host governments, on the other hand, must recognize that transnational corporations are by their nature not direct agents of social change but that given reasonably stable and equitable conditions under which to operate, they can make major contributions to Third World development goals.

Part IV

Appendixes

List of Participating Companies

UNITED STATES

1. Aluminum Company of America
2. AMAX Inc.
3. Atlantic Richfield Company
4. The Bendix Corporation
5. CPC International Inc.
6. The Carborundum Company
7. Caterpillar Tractor Co.
8. Celanese Corporation
9. Citibank, N.A.
10. The Coca-Cola Company
11. Cutler-Hammer Inc.
12. Deere & Company
13. Eli Lilly and Company
14. Exxon Corporation
15. The First National Bank of Chicago
16. General Electric Company
17. General Motors Corporation
18. The Hanna Mining Company
19. IBM Corporation
20. S. C. Johnson & Son, Inc.
21. Kimberly-Clark Corporation
22. Kraft, Inc.
23. Merck & Co., Inc.
24. RCA Corporation
25. Sears, Roebuck and Co.
26. Union Carbide Corporation
27. Westinghouse Electric Corporation

JAPAN

1. The Bank of Tokyo, Ltd.
2. Hitachi, Ltd.
3. Honda Motor Company, Ltd.
4. Komatsu, Ltd.
5. Matsushita Electric Industrial Company, Ltd.
6. Mitsubishi Corporation
7. Mitsubishi Heavy Industries, Ltd.
8. Mitsui and Company, Ltd.
9. Mitsui Mining and Smelting Co.
10. Nippon Electric Company, Ltd.
11. Nippon Steel Corporation
12. Nissan Motor Company
13. The Nomura Securities Company, Ltd.
14. Sumitomo Chemical Company, Ltd.
15. Taiyo Fishery Company, Ltd.
16. Toray Industries Inc.
17. Yoshida Kogyo K.K.

UNITED KINGDOM

1. Albright and Wilson
2. Barclays Bank
3. Booker McConnell
4. Courtaulds Ltd.
5. Guinness
6. Imperial Chemical Industries
7. Lucas Industries
8. Plessey
9. Rio Tinto Zinc Corporation
10. Smith and Nephew
11. Tootal
12. Tube Investments
13. Unilever

FEDERAL REPUBLIC OF GERMANY

Nine German firms participated in the project.

AUSTRALIA

1. Australian Consolidated Industries
2. Australian National Industries
3. Humes Limited
4. John Lysaght Ltd.
5. Nicholas International Ltd.
6. Thiess Holdings Ltd.
7. Wormald International Ltd.

SWEDEN

1. AGA AB
2. AB Alfa Laval
3. Granges AB
4. AB Nitro Nobel

5. Sandvik AB
6. Svenska Tandstick AB
7. AB Volvo

FRANCE

1. Lafarge
2. Moet-Hennessy
3. Pechincy-Ugine-Kuhlmann

4. Automobiles Peugeot S.A.
5. Scoa
6. Télémécanique Electrique

BELGIUM

1. Bekaert S.A.

ITALY

1. Société Internationale Pirelli S.A.

THE NETHERLANDS

1. N.V. Philips Gloeilampenfabriecken

SWITZERLAND

One Swiss firm participated in the project.

Factual
Questionnaire

The following brief and strictly factual questionnaire is designed to elicit in advance of the interview some basic information in capsule form about each Third World subsidiary of the parent firms to be interviewed. Its purpose is to make it possible to relate the responses to the questions in the interview survey to the location and type of subsidiaries controlled by each parent firm.

1. Name and location of subsidiary.
2. When was the subsidiary established?
3. Why was it established?
4. What products or services does it produce?
5. In what form did the subsidiary originate:
    a. takeover of existing concern?
    b. establishment of new company?
6. a. Is subsidiary wholly owned by parent company?
    b. If not wholly owned, how is ownership distributed among participants?
7. How large is the operation:
    a. number of employees?
    b. gross sales?
    c. capital investment (total assets and net worth)?

8. What percentage of total sales went to markets in:
   a. the host developing country?
   b. the home country?
   c. other?
9. What proportion of the dollar volume of raw materials and supplies was purchased from:
   a. local sources?
   b. the parent company?
   c. other affiliates of the parent company?
   d. other?
10. What types of incentives were provided by the host country:
    a. tariff or quota protection for subsidiary's products in host-country market?
    b. tariff reductions on imports of raw materials, components, or equipment?
    c. corporate income tax reduction or holiday?
    d. accelerated depreciation?
    e. investment credit?
    f. other?
11. What percentages of the following categories of the work force are local nationals:
    a. production workers?
    b. foremen and supervisors?
    c. clerical?
    d. sales?
    e. engineering?
    f. management?

Interview Questionnaire

A. FIELDS OF INVESTMENT

A-1. *a.* To what extent are the products or services produced by your firm in developing countries competitive with local and other foreign-owned enterprises? What problems arise as a result of this competition?

b. It is often claimed that emerging local entrepreneurs tend to be "smothered" by foreign affiliates of powerful multinational corporations. To what extent is this the case, and how can this danger be avoided?

A-2. Developing countries that are relatively large in terms of population and GNP have tended to pursue industrialization strategies of the import-substituting variety based on sheltered internal markets.

a. In your experience, have restrictions on access by foreign sources to the local markets of developing countries been an important reason for establishing foreign manufacturing subsidiaries in such countries?

b. How, in your opinion, does the local economy benefit from a policy of import substitution when the subsidy implicit in the protection of domestic producers accrues to a foreign-owned firm? What measures would you suggest to increase the local benefits from the operations of foreign-owned firms that are given protection in the local market?

c. Have sheltered markets in developing countries promoted the development by your companies of distinctive products and technologies for the local market?

A-3. How much freedom of entrepreneurial activity do you allow your subsidiary? For example, would you allow it to diversify into related products beyond the product line of the parent firm?

B. TYPES OF ARRANGEMENTS

B-1. Although viable alternatives to the classical foreign direct investment package may be most urgent in the natural resource field, developing countries are alleged to be interested in such alternatives for other sectors as well.

a. Do you find a general desire in developing countries to "unbundle" the foreign investment package of equity ownership, finance, plant management, technology, and market access?

b. How willing are you to respond to a developing country's wish to unbundle the foreign investment package?

c. In your opinion, would purchasing the ingredients separately lower the cost to the developing country of acquiring the foreign resources? (Answer for the various parts of the package and for the package as a whole.)

B-2. *a*. Do you have a general policy regarding the financing of operations in developing countries, such as minimizing your equity participation?

b. To what extent, for what reasons, and in what forms has your enterprise raised its capital from local sources?

c. If your company has used such local sources, do you think that your company's use has deprived local companies of financing?

B-3. The preference of developing countries for local participation in ownership and management of foreign subsidiaries is sometimes explained in terms of a greater readiness of local businessmen to conform to important national goals such as increasing employment or stimulating exports. The foreign partners, on the other hand, would be constrained by the overall corporate goals of the parent company.

a. How clearly are national goals articulated and understood in the developing countries in which you operate?

b. In your company's experience, how valid is the dichotomy between national and corporate goals?

c. To the extent that it is, what steps should be taken to reconcile your corporate interests with the national objectives?

d. Do you have any accounting or information system designed to show how your firm is serving the national priorities of the countries in which you operate?

B-4. Developing countries usually prefer joint ventures with local interests to wholly owned foreign subsidiaries and increasingly limit the proportion of ownership that may be acquired by the foreign firm. In some cases, a prescribed part of the foreign interest must eventually be sold to local buyers.

a. To what extent do such requirements deter the establishment by your company of foreign subsidiaries or reduce the flow of managerial and technical resources once the subsidiary has been established?

b. Are there ways of making the required domestic investment by local interests more acceptable to your company? If so, what would you suggest?

c. What role should host countries play in determining the composition of the management of foreign subsidiaries?

d. To what extent can multinational corporations reduce the onus of foreign operations by operating as joint ventures with other foreign firms and not just local interests (especially in the resource field)?

B-5. Almost a third of foreign subsidiaries in developing countries were established through the acquisition of going businesses by foreigners. Developing countries tend to frown on such acquisition, regarding it as a process of alienation of the domestic economy without offsetting benefits. In your experience, how has this method of establishing a subsidiary, compared with other methods, affected subsequent operations?

C. TRANSFER OF TECHNOLOGY

C-1. *a*. To what extent do your manufacturing and processing subsidiaries in developing countries adapt their products to local conditions such as the scale of the market, local raw material and skill availabilities, and the low cost of labor relative to that of capital?

b. To what extent do they adapt their processes and plant designs?

c. Do you have any central arrangements whereby adaptations in products, processes, and plant design are considered before technology is transferred to developing countries?

C-2. To what degree is your use of capital-intensive processes (in relation to the abundance of cheap labor in developing countries) a consequence of policies of the developing countries themselves (e.g., overvalued exchange rates that reduce the cost of imported equipment, tax concessions based on the amount of capital invested, and low or negative interest rates in real terms)?

C-3. Some developing countries require host-government approval of provisions in technology licensing agreements that they believe would restrict the normal growth of national industry.

a. To what extent do your licensing agreements include restrictive clauses, for example, obliging the licensee to purchase raw materials or components from the licensor, restricting exports, or "grant-back" provisions giving the licensor all rights to improvements?

b. To what extent have you experienced host-government requirements for approval of restrictive provisions, and how significant an obstacle to the transfer of technology are such requirements?

c. To what extent do you exercise quality control over the output of licensees? Does a lack of quality control result in restrictions on exports from subsidiaries? What would you suggest as a means to overcome impediments to granting wider marketing scope to licensees?

C-4. a. How important do you consider patent monopolies as conditions for transferring capital and technology to developing countries?

b. What types of limitations have you encountered in developing countries on the issuance or use of a patent monopoly? How did you react?

c. What policies should a developing country adopt to minimize the chance of abuse of this monopoly?

C-5. a. Have you established R and D facilities in developing countries? If so, what were your reasons?

b. If not, under what circumstances would your firm consider the establishment of such facilities?

c. Alternatively, would you contribute financially and technologically to a facility locally sponsored by government, an industry association, a university, or some other institution?

C-6. *a.* What sort of training facilities have you provided for local employees of your subsidiary, including, in particular, higher-level management training?

b. Would you consider a local national to head your subsidiary in a developing country?

c. How can the foreign enterprise and/or its home government contribute to the development of the human potential of the subsidiary?

d. Do you support any local or regional out-company management training programs such as the Asian Institute of Management in Manila or the Fundação Getulio Vargas in São Paolo?

e. What facilities do you provide for home-country training of host-country nationals?

f. Do you make any special effort to develop the adaptability of home-country employees to cultural differences when they are assigned to subsidiaries in developing countries?

C-7. *a.* To what extent do your subsidiaries subcontract activities to local manufacturers?

b. In what ways are the local manufacturers assisted in this regard?

D. OTHER HOST-COUNTRY POLICIES

D-1. *a.* Has your company benefited from exemptions or reductions of income and other taxes, investment grants, or other assistance provided by developing countries to foreign firms during their early years?

b. Have such incentives really been effective in increasing your investment in developing countries?

c. It is sometimes claimed that the practice tends primarily to encourage mutually disadvantageous competition in incentives among developing countries trying to attract foreign investors. How can this problem best be met?

D-2. Host governments frequently complain that foreign subsidiaries understate their local income and therefore underpay their local taxes because of practices related to transfer pricing, royalty payments, and administrative charges between affiliated companies.

a. Do you think this practice is widespread?

b. How can host developing countries monitor such intracompany transactions more effectively?

c. What should home countries do to prevent abuses in transfer pricing?

d. Do you think that bilateral or multilateral arrangements are necessary or feasible to regulate such practices?

D-3. It is sometimes stated that the issue of intracorporate pricing is exaggerated where, as in the case of U.S. companies, the home government allows a credit for income taxes paid to the host government. So long as the tax rate in the host country is lower than that of the home country, there should be no incentive on the part of the foreign subsidiary to minimize income in the host country. Does not an incentive remain to *maximize* income in the host country where, again as in the case of U.S. companies, the foreign subsidiary is allowed to defer home-country taxes until its income is repatriated to the parent company?

D-4. Host governments tend to raise questions about the legitimacy of deductions of interest as a business expense when a subsidiary borrows from its parent. Such transactions are sometimes regarded as equivalent to an equity investment and therefore not entitled to deductions. Alternatively, a withholding tax imposed by host countries has been proposed on interest paid by affiliates. Because interest can at times absorb a large part of operating income, how can host countries ensure that intracorporate lending does not become a device for circumventing local corporate income taxes?

D-5. Host governments commonly complain that certain types of foreign operations have an enclave character in the sense that they have few backward or forward linkages to the domestic economy. Backward linkages refer to the purchase of local inputs; forward linkages, to the domestic use of the firm's output in further productive operations. Examples of inadequate backward linkages are the assembly of automobiles from imported components and the packaging of pharmaceuticals from imported materials. Examples of inadequate forward linkages are the export of ores or logs without further local processing into metals or plywood. The processing of imported goods for reexport is illustrative of both types of enclave operations.

a. What experience have you had with host-government efforts to link foreign operations more closely with the local economy through requirements for progressive increases in the local value-added content of manufactured products or incentives for the further local processing of primary materials?

b. If host governments forbid the export of primary materials in unprocessed form, what effect do you think it will have on their development?

D-6. a. What experience have you had with efforts by developing countries to induce local manufacturing subsidiaries to export rather than to produce solely for the local market?

b. To what extent does this objective conflict with the policies of your company, and how can the two be reconciled?

D-7. A number of host countries have extensive legislation and regulations on employment conditions and industrial relations, for example, requirements for the training and upgrading of the labor force; limitations on the number and type of foreign nationals that may be employed; rules for consultation with government and employee representatives on changes in operations affecting the livelihood of employees; and limitations on the right to discharge workers or to threaten, in the context of labor negotiations, to transfer an operating unit from the country. What requirements of this sort has your company faced, and how has it reacted to them?

D-8. A number of host governments have written the Calvo Doctrine into their foreign investment law. Under this doctrine, countries seek to ensure that foreign subsidiaries of multinational corporations settle with local governments within local laws and not appeal to their home governments for protection or support in case of disputes.

a. How have your company's decisions been influenced by the host government's adherence to the Calvo Doctrine?

b. Is the disincentive effect of the Calvo Doctrine removed or mitigated by the adoption of a policy of "national treatment" (i.e., nondiscriminatory treatment in comparison with national enterprises)?

D-9. a. Can the fear of host-country nationalization of foreign enterprises be mitigated by the inclusion in its foreign investment law of procedures for compensation, including a specific formula for determining the level of such compensation?

b. Can you give an example of what you consider a desirable arrangement now in effect?

D-10. a. Has your company been pressured to do things for reasons of internal politics in host countries? How did you react?

b. What would you suggest as the best way to discourage such pressures?

D-11. A developing country typically wants to avoid long-run commitments to a foreign firm that would limit its freedom of action in the face of an unpredictable future. A multinational firm, on the other hand, looks for stability and assurance against arbitrary changes in the conditions of its operation. How can those two interests best be reconciled (e.g., by provision for periodic renegotiation of contracts)?

D-12. In order of importance, what do you regard as the most serious deterrents to foreign investment in developing countries?

E. HOME-COUNTRY POLICIES

E-1. a. Should home countries provide or continue inducements for their firms to establish subsidiaries abroad in developing countries?

b. If so, should the inducements be of general applicability, or should they be applied selectively to those countries or those types of investment where promotion is deemed to be in the mutual interest of both home and host country?

E-2. Several industrial countries accord investments in the developing countries more favorable tax treatment than investments in other foreign countries. (For example, prior to the Tax Reform Act of 1976, the United States did not require "grossing up" of dividends paid by subsidiaries, and capital gains treatment has been given for retained earnings when a subsidiary is liquidated after ten years.)

a. What type of inducements does your home country offer to promote investment in developing countries?

b. How significant are such provisions in channeling your investment to developing countries?

c. Should they be continued?

E-3. A number of home countries provide for deferral of income tax on earnings of subsidiaries abroad until the profits are repatriated to the parent company. This provision has three effects that require careful assessment in terms of the objective of promoting social and economic development in the Third World: (1) Deferral subsidizes the reinvestment of foreign earnings (net of host-country tax) by converting such earnings in host countries with tax rates lower than the home-country rate into an interest-free loan to the firm. (2) Deferral provides an incentive for firms to manipulate their transfer prices so as to shift income into low-tax countries. (If all foreign incomes were taxed currently, firms would be more indifferent to the locus of their earnings.) (3) Deferral permits host countries to attract foreign direct investment by offering tax rates lower than home-country rates. (Without deferral, the home country would siphon off any difference between a lower foreign tax rate and its own corporate tax rate.)

a. Is deferral a feature of your home country's taxation of foreign investment?

b. If so, how would you assess the consequences of deferral on your operations abroad, particularly in relation to the three effects mentioned above?

E-4. Some home governments provide various forms of insurance to facilitate a flow of capital and other resources to the developing countries.

a. How effective is such insurance in inducing foreign investment in developing countries?

b. Should the insurer be more selective, perhaps limiting its operations to the poorer countries that are unable to attract private foreign capital on their own?

c. Should the insurer avoid inherently unstable wholly owned equity investments in natural resources in favor of management contracts or perhaps joint ventures?

E-5. Tensions with host countries have resulted from efforts by home countries to apply national laws and regulations to foreign subsidiaries in such fields as antitrust and capital controls.

a. What has been your experience with such efforts to extend home-country jurisdiction?

b. What limits should be set on the jurisdictional reach of domestic law as it affects the operations of subsidiaries abroad?

E-6. *a*. What steps might home governments take in order to ensure fair treatment by host countries of foreign investment?

b. If a host country expropriates foreign property without prompt, adequate, and effective compensation, should the home government resort to any of the following punitive measures: suspension of foreign aid to the expropriating country, negative vote on loans being considered by multinational development banks, or denial of trade preferences?

c. How effective are such measures likely to be?

E-7. *a*. What should the role of home governments be in issues arising between multinational enterprises and host governments?

b. How closely should subsidiaries keep in touch with their embassies abroad in the absence of crisis situations?

E-8. *a*. Has your company refrained from investing in or trading with other countries because of considerations related to the political system or situation prevailing in any such country?

b. If so, has your decision been guided by home-country legislation, regulation, public opinion, or personal judgment?

c. Do you regard such political considerations in investment or trading policies as appropriate or reasonable, and should regulations be adopted if they do not now exist?

E-9. *a*. Should home governments attempt to legislate or otherwise regulate the conduct of their companies abroad to ensure against corrupt practices in host countries?

b. Should home governments attempt to discourage investor involvement in local politics in order to obtain preferential treatment?

c. Should corrupt practices be treated primarily through requirements for disclosure of financial information to regulatory bodies?

d. What should companies or industries do about such practices on a voluntary basis?

F. INTERNATIONAL PROGRAMS AND ARRANGEMENTS

F-1. Three proposals for increasing the flow of private capital to developing countries have been put forward by the United States at recent international meetings: the creation of an international investment trust to mobilize portfolio capital for investment in local enterprises in the Third World, an increase in the capital of the International Finance Corporation, the arm of the World Bank dedicated to enlisting private capital in support of development projects in the Third World; and the creation of a new International Resources Bank to guarantee foreign private loan capital invested in resource projects in developing countries.

a. Do you favor these or other initiatives for mobilizing foreign private capital for developing countries outside the traditional framework of equity investment through multinational corporations?

b. How effective are such initiatives likely to be?

F-2. Many developing countries now borrow large sums in the international capital markets, particularly in the form of syndicated Eurocurrency bank loans. Bond issues in national capital markets, however, are subject to a variety of constraints such as foreign exchange regulations in Europe and legal restrictions imposed by states on institutional investors in the United States.

a. What can be done to widen the access of indigenous firms and national governments or state governments in developing countries to the bond markets in the industrial countries?

b. Should some sort of international guarantee mechanism be established?

F-3. A set of OECD guidelines for transnational enterprises (and home and host governments) has been adopted by OECD member countries. A U.N. effort is now under way to establish guidelines applicable to the operations of multinational corporations in developing countries as well.

a. Do you support the current U.N. effort to establish guidelines for the operations of multinational corporations in developing countries?

b. Should such an effort be supplemented by unilateral home- or host-government action or by multinationals voluntarily, either singly or in concert?

F-4. a. Should the OECD countries cooperate with an effort now getting under way in the United Nations to draft a code of conduct that would apply to foreign direct investment in the developing countries?

b. How should the OECD countries react to the demand of the developing countries that such a code should be mandatory rather than voluntary, and applicable only to multinational enterprises, not to domestic enterprises or to governments?

F-5. a. Should an international effort be made to harmonize national tax policies affecting multinational enterprises?

b. Should provisions be included limiting tax incentives for foreign investors, such as tax holidays, accelerated depreciation, and investment credits?

F-6. a. Because tariffs and other forms of protection are also used as special incentives, should some degree of harmonization be sought in this policy area as well?

b. Where protective trade measures are mainly used to offset overvalued exchange rates, what sort of parallel action would need to be taken on the monetary side?

F-7. The U.N. Group of Eminent Persons has called for work to begin on an international antitrust code. Do you agree that rules on restrictive business practices should be negotiated internationally to deal with such practices as export restrictions, market allocation, and price collusion?

F-8. A number of industrial countries now provide government insurance against the noncommercial risks of private foreign investment in developing countries.

a. Should such insurance be multilateralized to the maximum extent?

b. Should it include financial participation by developing countries to reflect a mutual stake in encouraging foreign investment in the service of development?

F-9. The World Bank's International Centre for the Settlement of Investment Disputes provides machinery for conciliation and arbitration. Thus far, however, its work has been very limited, mainly because of the nonparticipation of many countries, especially in Latin America, on the grounds that disputes in their countries should be settled under national jurisdiction. What can be done to widen the use of international fact-finding and arbitral procedures in disputes between host governments and multinational enterprises?

APPENDIX D

Statistical Profile of the Affiliates

This appendix presents a statistical description and analysis of the Third World affiliates of the participating parent companies. Its purpose is twofold: to describe certain key characteristics of the affiliates and to explore some tentative comparisons in light of the responses presented in Part II and summarized in Part III.

All parent companies participating in the interview survey were asked to respond to a brief, confidential factual questionnaire (see Appendix B) on each of their affiliates operating in a developing country. The original purpose of this questionnaire was to relate the answers to the interview questions to the type, location, and other characteristics of the affiliates of the parent firm.

As the questionnaires were returned, however, it became clear that a considerable body of valuable data about the transnational affiliates had been assembled. Although the responses were in many cases incomplete, it appeared useful and informative to organize and present the data in summary form and to apply to them some simple statistical analysis.

As can be seen in Table 1, the degree of response to the factual questionnaire varied greatly. A number of parent companies did not comply with our request, either because of the difficulty of compiling the data or because of an unwillingness to reveal private data even on a confidential

Note: Robert Fisher was principally responsible for the preparation of this appendix. Valuable advice and assistance were provided by Professors James Riedel and Harold Fassberg of The Johns Hopkins University.

Table 1. Response to the Factual Questionnaire

Home Country of Parent Firm	Total Number of Firms Interviewed	Number of Parent Firms Submitting Factual Questionnaires	Number of Subsidiaries for which Factual Questionnaires Were Prepared
1. United States	27	17	188
2. Japan	17	15	84
3. Australia	7	7	41
4. Sweden	7	7	41
5. France	6	5	31
6. United Kingdom	13	2	7
7. Belgium	1	1	5
8. Italy	1	1	5
9. Germany	9	—[a]	—[a]
10. Netherlands	1	0	0
11. Switzerland	1	0	0
Total	90	55	402

[a] The 9 participating German parent companies returned a total of 69 questionnaires to the German counterpart organization, CEPES. The terms under which these companies agreed to participate preluded CEPES from forwarding these questionnaires to CED for inclusion in this appendix.

basis. In addition, several transnationals provided responses for only a representative sample of their subsidiaries or only partially completed the questionnaire.

A total of 402 fully or partially filled-out questionnaires were returned. Where companies did not provide complete data, their responses were supplemented by published material, such as annual reports and, in the case of the American firms, 10-K forms.

The data from all sources pertained to twenty-six basic characteristics, as listed in Table 2.

THE AFFILIATES: AN OVERVIEW

A comparison of selected characteristics for all the affiliates is presented in Table 3. For the purposes of this comparison, the subsidiaries were divided into three groups. Both the American and the Japanese transnationals provided sufficient data (in terms of completed factual questionnaires) to allow the affiliates of the parent firms of each country to be considered as separate sample sets. The samples from the other home countries were either too small or too incomplete to permit individual, country-by-country analysis. The data for Australia, Belgium, France, Germany, Italy, the Netherlands, Sweden, and the United Kingdom were therefore combined into the "other" category.

One of the more interesting findings (Table 3, line 1) is that Japanese firms appear on average to have started investing directly in developing countries about ten years later than U.S. companies. This may be partially due to the fact that Japan's economic development lagged behind

Table 2. List and Description of Characteristics of Affiliates on which Data Were Collected

Group I [a]	Description [b]
1. Age of affiliate	Number of years since affiliate was first established or acquired. Base year is 1978.
2. Parent ownership	Percentage of affiliate's equity owned by the parent firm.
3. Employees	Total number of employees of the affiliate.
4. Annual sales	Dollar value of an affiliate's annual sales.
5. Total assets	Total current and fixed assets less depreciation.
6. Net worth	Stockholders' equity plus retained earnings.
7. Sales within host market	Sales within host country as percentage of total sales.
8. Sales to home market	Sales to home country of parent firm as percentage of total sales.
9. Purchases, local	Raw materials and supplies purchased within the host country as percentage of total purchases.
10. Purchases, parent	Raw materials and supplies purchased from the parent company as percentage of total purchases.
11. Purchases, affiliates	Raw materials and supplies purchased from other affiliates of the parent firm as percentage of total purchases.
12. Purchases, other	Raw materials and supplies purchased from other sources as percentage of total purchases.
13. Locals, production workers	Local nationals as percentage of total number of production workers.
14. Locals, foremen	Local nationals as percentage of total number of foremen.
15. Locals, clerical	Local nationals as percentage of total number of clerical personnel.
16. Locals, sales	Local nationals as percentage of total number of sales personnel.
17. Locals, engineering	Local nationals as percentage of total number of engineers employed.
18. Locals, management	Local nationals as percentage of total number of managerial personnel.

Table 2 (*continued*)

Group II [c]	Question
1. Takeovers	Was the affiliate acquired as an existing local enterprise?
2. New starts	Was the affiliate a newly established firm?
3. Tariff or quota protection	Did the affiliate receive tariff or quota protection from the host country as an incentive to invest?
4. Tariff reduction on imports	Did the affiliate receive a tariff reduction on its imports of raw materials, components, or equipment as an incentive to invest?
5. Tax incentives	Did the affiliate receive a tax reduction or holiday from the host country as an inducement to invest?
6. Accelerated depreciation	Did the affiliate receive accelerated depreciation from the host country as an investment incentive?
7. Investment credits	Did the affiliate receive investment credits as an investment incentive?
8. Other incentives	Did the affiliate receive any incentives other than those listed above to invest in the host country?

[a] Group I includes characteristics for which quantitative information was received for each affiliate.

[b] Data are generally for the year prior to the interview. Interviews were conducted over a three-year period from mid-1976 to mid-1979; most were conducted during 1978.

[c] Group II includes characteristics for which nonquantitative information was received for each affiliate.

that of the United States. Another contributing factor may have been a hesitation on the part of the Japanese to move too soon after World War II into the formerly occupied areas of eastern and southern Asia.

The historical reluctance of U.S. companies to enter into joint ventures is reflected in the statistics on the proportion of a subsidiary's equity owned by the parent firm (Table 3, line 2). The average for U.S. transnationals is 86 percent, compared with 73 percent for other, mainly European, firms. The relative willingness of Japanese companies to enter into joint ventures is indicated by the Japanese average of 50 percent. As latecomers in establishing foreign affiliates, the Japanese may well have faced greater host-country pressure for joint ventures. (See Chapter 7 for a discussion of joint ventures.)

Japanese subsidiaries and branches are significantly smaller than those of U.S. transnationals as measured by the number of employees and total annual sales per affiliate (Table 3, lines 3 and 4). The affiliates of other transnationals do not show statistically significant differences in

Table 3. Survey of Selected Characteristics for All Affiliates

Group I: Characteristic[a]	Number of Observations[b]	Mean	Coefficient of Variation[c]	Range Low	Range High
1. Age of affiliate (number of years)					
United States	180	18.1	0.7	1	62
Japan	84	8.5**[d]	0.6	1	24
Other	120	20.2	1.0	1	153
2. Parent ownership (percent)					
United States	163	85.8	0.2	31.0	100.0
Japan	84	50.5**	0.6	2.0	100.0
Other	576	73.0**	0.5	5.0	100.0
3. Employees (number)					
United States	154	876	2.5	1	19,253
Japan	83	525*	1.2	4	3,260
Other	215	1,114	2.9	1	37,768
4. Annual sales (millions of dollars)					
United States	34	34.8	2.8	0.1	761.0
Japan	55	17.0*	1.3	0.3	120.5
Other	144	23.4	2.9	0.03	556.6
5. Sales within host market (percent)					
United States	124	81.8	0.4	0.0	100.0
Japan	57	74.7	0.5	0.0	100.0
Other	88	90.1*	0.3	0.0	100.0
6. Sales to home country (percent)					
United States	123	3.4	5.1	0.0	100.0
Japan	57	12.3*	2.3	0.0	100.0
Other	88	0.5*	8.0	0.0	37.0
7. Purchases, local (percent)					
United States	95	45.9	0.7	0.0	100.0
Japan	50	37.6	1.0	0.0	100.0
Other	72	34.7*	1.1	0.0	100.0
8. Purchases, parent (percent)					
United States	78	20.9	1.3	0.0	90.0
Japan	50	46.7**	0.9	0.0	100.0
Other	72	42.3**	1.0	0.0	100.0
9. Purchases, affiliates (percent)					
United States	77	14.7	1.8	0.0	95.0
Japan	50	5.2*	3.7	0.0	100.0
Other	72	3.9**	2.5	0.0	45.0
10. Purchases, other (percent)					
United States	77	17.0	1.5	0.0	97.0
Japan	50	10.5	2.5	0.0	100.0
Other	72	19.1	1.5	0.0	100.0

Table 3 *(continued)*

Group I: Characteristic[a]	Number of Observations[b]	Mean	Coefficient of Variation[c]	Range Low	High
11. Locals, production workers (percent)					
United States	121	97.9	0.1	0.0	100.0
Japan	57	95.8	0.2	0.0	100.0
Other	68	97.5	0.2	0.0	100.0
12. Locals, foremen (percent)					
United States	121	98.2	0.1	0.0	100.0
Japan	55	86.2**	0.3	0.0	100.0
Other	69	94.0*	0.2	0.0	100.0
13. Locals, clerical (percent)					
United States	124	98.7	0.1	0.0	100.0
Japan	61	92.4*	0.2	5.0	100.0
Other	69	94.0*	0.2	0.0	100.0
14. Locals, sales (percent)					
United States	117	95.4	0.2	0.0	100.0
Japan	55	82.2**	0.4	0.0	100.0
Other	68	91.5	0.2	0.0	100.0
15. Locals, engineering (percent)					
United States	114	97.1	0.1	0.0	100.0
Japan	50	72.1**	0.5	0.0	100.0
Other	69	87.8**	0.3	0.0	100.0
16. Locals, management (percent)					
United States	125	83.9	0.3	0.0	100.0
Japan	56	59.5**	0.6	0.0	100.0
Other	66	50.2**	0.8	0.0	100.0

Group II: Characteristic	Number of Observations	Percent of Total
17. Takeovers		
United States	165	17.6
Japan	80	15.0
Other	97	22.7
18. New starts		
United States	165	82.4
Japan	80	85.0
Other	97	77.3
19. Tariff or quota protection		
United States	110	30.9
Japan	61	32.8
Other	78	19.2
20. Tariff reduction on imports		
United States	110	34.6
Japan	61	62.3
Other	78	10.3

Table 3 *(continued)*

Group II: Characteristic	Number of Observations	Percent of Total
21. Tax incentives		
United States	110	30.0
Japan	61	54.5
Other	78	30.8
22. Accelerated depreciation		
United States	110	20.0
Japan	61	18.0
Other	78	10.3
23. Investment credit		
United States	110	10.0
Japan	61	16.4
Other	78	5.1
24. Other incentives		
United States	110	22.7
Japan	61	6.6
Other	78	7.7

Note: The findings for each country group (United States, Japan, Other) were computed for each characteristic using all available data.

[a] See Table 2 for a description of each characteristic.

[b] The number of observations indicates the number of affiliates for which information was provided on a given characteristic.

[c] The coefficient of variation is the standard deviation divided by the mean. It is a measure of the relative dispersion of the observations around the mean. The larger the coefficient, the greater the degree of variation.

[d] Through the use of t-statistics, the significance of the difference between the means of two sample sets can be tested. This is done by comparing the difference between the means with a measure of the variation from the mean within each sample set. This procedure takes into account the size of the samples in determining the significance of differences between the means. Because the purpose is simply to illustrate the types of analysis that can be done, the mean values of one group of affiliates (the U.S. sample) have been taken as the base, and the means of the remaining groups have been compared with them. Similar comparisons of other pairs of means can be made by using other bases.

* Probability of significant differences in group means is 90 percent.

** Probability of significant differences in group means is 99 percent.

size from those of the U.S. companies. The Japanese affiliates also show a much lower level of variability in size than either the U.S. or the other companies do.

According to many transnationals, a key motivating force in the decision to establish manufacturing facilities in developing countries has been the desire to enter or preserve a market that has become or has threatened to become restricted or closed to exports from the home base because of import-substitution policies adopted by host countries (see

Chapter 6). This fact may very well explain the large share of the dollar volume of total sales that is accounted for by sales within the host country for each group of subsidiaries (Table 3, line 5). Affiliates of Japanese transnationals sell an average of 75 percent of their total production within the host country; U.S. subsidiaries, about 82 percent; and those of other transnationals, just over 90 percent.[1] The latter is significantly higher than the average for U.S. affiliates.

Affiliates of transnational enterprises depend on a variety of sources for their purchased inputs (see Chapter 8). As a percentage of the total dollar volume of raw materials and supplies used by affiliates in developing countries, the share of local inputs used by American firms is significantly greater than that of the other transnationals, although not of the Japanese (Table 3, line 7). The share of local inputs for the American companies averages 46 percent; for the Japanese affiliates, 38 percent; and for the other firms, 35 percent. American subsidiaries receive only 20.9 percent of their inputs from their parent companies. Non-U.S. affiliates, however, rely on the parent company to a much larger extent for their inputs (Table 3, line 8). The Japanese affiliates receive 46.7 percent of their raw materials and supplies from their parent companies, and affiliates of other transnationals obtain 42.3 percent from this source.

Several points stand out in the statistics on the percentage of local nationals in the affiliates' work forces. The first is that in most categories—production workers, foremen, clerical staff, salesmen, and engineers—local nationals constitute the overwhelming majority of the work force (Table 3, lines 11 to 15). These data are fully consistent with the responses given to the interview questionnaire (see Chapter 8). In general, U.S. subsidiaries show a significantly stronger tendency to use local employees than non-American affiliates do (except for production workers, where the higher U.S. proportion of local employees is not significant, and sales personnel, where the U.S. proportion of local employees is not significantly greater than the proportion for other companies).

For all groups, the share of local personnel in management is lower than it is in other job categories (Table 3, line 16). The drop is much more pronounced for non-U.S. affiliates. Local nationals account for 84 percent of the managers in U.S. subsidiaries, 59 percent in the Japanese, and just over 50 percent in affiliates of other transnationals.

---

[1] Within each sample set, the majority of the affiliates are manufacturing firms.

The data on takeovers and new starts support the transnationals' assertions that they generally have little experience in acquiring existing local businesses (see Chapter 7). New starts outnumber takeovers by a margin of more than five to one for Japanese companies, four to one for U.S. transnationals, and three to one for other firms (Table 3, lines 17 and 18).

Transnationals differ by home-country origin in the extent to which they benefit from host-country investment incentives (Table 3, lines 19 to 24; see also Chapter 9). The Japanese appear to benefit most frequently from tariff reductions on imports of raw materials, components, or equipment, as well as from various tax incentives: 62 percent of the Japanese affiliates have used the former and 54 percent the latter. In comparison, about 35 percent of the U.S. affiliates have received tariff reductions on imported inputs, and 30 percent have received tax incentives. A roughly equal proportion of U.S. and Japanese firms (31 and 33 percent, respectively) also took advantage of tariff or quota protection on their final products. The data suggest that with the exception of tax incentives, subsidiaries of other transnational enterprises are generally granted far less in the way of investment inducements. For example, only 10 percent of these firms were granted tariff reductions on imports, and only 19 percent received tariff or quota protection on their final products.

U.S. AFFILIATES

As presented in Table 3, the data provide a broad description of transnational affiliates according to the nationality of the parent company. For the purposes of more detailed analysis, the data can be classified to allow comparisons on such bases as industrial sector or geographic location of the affiliates.

Because the U.S. sample includes the largest number of completed factual questionnaires, it has been chosen as the set of subsidiaries on which this discussion will focus. Given sufficient data, a similar analysis could be carried out for any other sample set.

Industrial Sector

U.S. subsidiaries were first classified according to five industrial sectors: extractive; manufacturing, consumer goods; manufacturing, intermediate goods; manufacturing, capital goods; and service. Sufficient information was received about 178 out of a total of 188 affiliates in the U.S. sample to allow them to be categorized in this fashion. Of the 178 firms, 10 were in the extractive sector, 115 in the consumer goods sector, 11 in the intermediate goods sector, 21 in the capital goods sector, and 21 in the service sector.

Analysis was performed on the data for particular characteristics. A comparison, by sector, of the mean, coefficient of variation, and range of observations for each characteristic is presented in Table 4.

As these data indicate, the differences between the mean values of the base category (the consumer goods sector) and those of the other industrial groups in the sample are not statistically significant for most of the characteristics analyzed. Yet the interview responses frequently revealed sharp divergencies of views among executives of firms in different industrial fields. This seeming incongruence can be explained by the fact that the interviews elicited attitudes and perceptions of businessmen on a much wider range of subjects than those on which factual data were obtained. Where the interview responses and the factual data relate to the same subject, as in the case of the employment of local nationals in managerial positions, the data confirm what was stated by the interview respondents.

Although the sector means showed no significant differences for most characteristics, extractive affiliates did diverge sharply from the norm in several cases. For example, compared with consumer goods subsidiaries, they average a significantly higher level of total sales, $105.1 million annually, compared with $24.5 million (Table 4, line 4).

On the relative importance of sales within the host market and sales back to the home market, the extractive firms show, as one would expect, a pattern opposite to that of the consumer goods manufacturing companies (Table 4, lines 7 and 8). Sales within the host country account for 81.2 percent of total sales of consumer goods affiliates and only 21.6 percent for extractive subsidiaries. On the other hand, exports back to the home country are only 1.9 percent of total sales for the consumer goods sector but 58.6 percent for extractive affiliates. In each case, the differences are statistically significant.[2]

---

[2] Actually, the percentages of sales to host and home countries for extractive firms show statistically significant differences compared with those of each of the remaining industrial sectors.

Table 4. Sector Distribution of Selected Characteristics for U.S. Affiliates

Characteristic[a]	Number of Observations[b]	Mean	Coefficient of Variation[c]	Range Low	High
1. Age of affiliate (number of years)					
Manufacturing, consumer goods	111	17.5	0.8	2	54
Manufacturing, intermediate goods	11	13.4	0.7	4	32
Manufacturing, capital goods	17	18.9	0.9	3	59
Extractive	10	18.6	0.9	1	62
Service	21	20.6	0.7	3	56
2. Parent ownership (percent)					
Manufacturing, consumer goods	90	85.8	0.2	31.0	100.0
Manufacturing, intermediate goods	11	79.3	0.4	32.0	100.0
Manufacturing, capital goods	21	76.7	0.3	40.0	100.0
Extractive	10	90.0	0.3	32.0	100.0
Service	21	91.1	0.2	40.0	100.0
3. Employees (number)					
Manufacturing, consumer goods	83	701	3.2	8	19,253
Manufacturing, intermediate goods	11	476	1.3	20	2,137
Manufacturing, capital goods	20	1,820	1.9	20	12,000
Extractive	10	1,090	1.5	1	5,090
Service	21	1,021	1.6	2	6,263
4. Annual sales (millions of dollars)					
Manufacturing, consumer goods	83	24.5	3.4	0.1	750.0
Manufacturing, intermediate goods	9	16.7	1.2	2.0	60.0
Manufacturing, capital goods	18	40.3	1.7	0.6	225.0
Extractive	4	105.1*[d]	0.8	1.2	169.0
Service	19	68.6	2.5	0.4	761.0
5. Total assets (millions of dollars)					
Manufacturing, consumer goods	68	25.7	5.2	0.1	600.0
Manufacturing, intermediate goods	8	24.8	1.5	0.4	112.0
Manufacturing, capital goods	17	21.2	2.8	0.1	241.3
Extractive	6	101.2	1.3	5.0	286.0
Service	19	32.0	1.5	0.05	152.0
6. Net worth (millions of dollars)					
Manufacturing, consumer goods	29	6.2	2.0	0.05	61.5
Manufacturing, intermediate goods	4	9.7	0.9	0.7	17.5

Table 4 *(continued)*

Characteristic[a]	Number of Observations[b]	Mean	Coefficient of Variation[c]	Range Low	High
Manufacturing, capital goods	10	6.2	2.2	0.2	45.1
Extractive	0	—	—	—	—
Service	11	12.4	1.5	0.05	36.5
7. Sales within host market (percent)					
Manufacturing, consumer goods	64	81.2	0.4	0.0	100.0
Manufacturing, intermediate goods	11	89.9	0.3	13.0	100.0
Manufacturing, capital goods	17	81.4	0.4	0.0	100.0
Extractive	5	21.6**	2.0	0.0	100.0
Service	18	87.2	0.3	12.0	100.0
8. Sales to home market (percent)					
Manufacturing, consumer goods	64	1.9	6.6	0.0	100.0
Manufacturing, intermediate goods	11	0.1	3.5	0.0	1.5
Manufacturing, capital goods	16	0.2	3.9	0.0	3.0
Extractive	5	58.6*	0.9	0.0	100.0
Service	18	0.0	0.0	0.0	0.0
9. Locals, management (percent)					
Manufacturing, consumer goods	65	83.6	0.3	17.0	100.0
Manufacturing, intermediate goods	11	90.6	0.2	37.0	100.0
Manufacturing, capital goods	19	80.8	0.4	0.0	100.0
Extractive	8	82.9	0.3	38.0	100.0
Service	14	84.1	0.3	0.0	100.0

Note: The findings for each industrial group were computed for each characteristic using all available data.

[a] See Table 2 for description of each characteristic.

[b] See Table 3, note b, for definition.

[c] See Table 3, note c, for definition.

[d] Through the use of t-statistics, the significance of the difference between the means of two sample sets can be tested. This is done by comparing the difference between the means with a measure of the variation from the mean within each sample set. This procedure takes into account the size of the samples in determining the significance of the differences between the means. Because the purpose is simply to illustrate the types of analysis that can be done, the mean values of one group of affiliates (the manufacturing consumer goods sector) have been taken as the base, and the means of the remaining groups have been compared with them. The consumer goods sector was chosen as the base because it is the largest group of affiliates. Similar comparisons of other pairs of means can be made by using other bases.

* Probability of significant differences in group means is 90 percent.

** Probability of significant differences in group means is 99 percent.

Geographic Location

The data were also analyzed according to the geographic locations of the U.S. parent companies' affiliates: Latin America and the Caribbean, Asia, Africa, and the Middle East and North Africa. Data were available on 188 subsidiaries: 107 in Latin America and the Caribbean, 56 in Asia, 15 in Africa, and 10 in the Middle East and North Africa.[3] A comparison of selected characteristics for these affiliates is presented in Table 5.

A brief review of the table reveals that for each characteristic, the mean values of the Latin American affiliates differ significantly from those of most of the remaining regions. As would be expected, U.S. firms tended to invest in Latin America before they established affiliates in other areas of the Third World (Table 5, line 1). The average age of Latin American affiliates is 21.5 years, compared with 16.7 years for Asian, 7.9 years for African, and 7.2 years for Middle Eastern affiliates.

In addition to having invested earlier in Latin America than in other Third World regions, U.S. parent companies tend to own significantly more equity in their Latin American affiliates (91.2 percent) than in either their Asian (78.6 percent) or their African (73.3 percent) subsidiaries (Table 5, line 2).

Latin American affiliates are in most cases significantly larger than those located in other regions as measured by the number of employees, total annual sales, total assets, and net worth per affiliate (Table 5, lines 3 to 6). Total annual sales for Latin American subsidiaries average almost $49 million. For affiliates located in the Middle East, the average level of sales is $18.5 million; for those situated in Asia, $15.9 million. African subsidiaries average only $4 million in sales, a level significantly smaller than that of subsidiaries located in any of the other regions.[4]

With respect to the total dollar value of sales accounted for by sales within the host country, the average for subsidiaries located in Latin America is just under 86 percent (Table 5, line 7). The average for Asian affiliates is significantly lower, 69.5 percent; and for subsidiaries located in Africa, the average is significantly higher, 97.7 percent. At the same time, Latin American subsidiaries are the only affiliates reporting any appreciable level of sales back to the home country (Table 5, line 8).

---

[3] Latin America and the Caribbean are hereafter referred to as Latin America; the Middle East and North Africa are referred to as the Middle East.

[4] For each of the size characteristics listed, African subsidiaries are significantly smaller than Latin American or Asian affiliates.

Table 5. Survey of Selected Characteristics for U.S. Affiliates, by Geographic Region

Characteristic [a]	Number of Observations[b]	Mean	Coefficient of Variation[c]	Range Low	Range High
1. Age of affiliate (number of years)					
Latin America	100	21.5	0.7	1	62
Asia	55	16.7* [d]	0.7	3	48
Africa	15	7.9**	0.5	2	15
Middle East	10	7.2**	0.5	3	16
2. Parent ownership (percent)					
Latin America	97	91.2	0.2	32.0	100.0
Asia	47	78.6**	0.3	31.0	100.0
Africa	12	73.3**	0.3	49.0	100.0
Middle East	7	80.7	0.3	45.0	100.0
3. Employees (number)					
Latin America	94	1,153	2.3	1	19,253
Asia	43	560*	2.6	12	9,683
Africa	11	127**	0.7	20	298
Middle East	6	168**	0.7	8	325
4. Annual sales (millions of dollars)					
Latin America	81	48.7	2.5	0.4	761.0
Asia	42	15.9*	2.0	0.1	168.3
Africa	11	4.0**	0.6	0.5	7.5
Middle East	6	18.5*	1.1	0.5	50.0
5. Total assets (millions of dollars)					
Latin America	79	35.4	2.3	0.05	600.0
Asia	35	19.6	2.4	0.7	260.4
Africa	9	4.2**	0.5	0.8	6.8
Middle East	5	12.7*	1.7	0.01	50.0
6. Net worth (millions of dollars)					
Latin America	33	9.8	1.4	0.05	61.5
Asia	25	4.7*	1.9	0.2	45.1
Africa	3	0.4**	0.6	0.2	0.7
Middle East	1	2.3*	0.0	2.3	2.3
7. Sales within host market (percent)					
Latin America	78	85.9	0.3	0.0	100.0
Asia	35	69.5*	0.6	0.0	100.0
Africa	7	97.7**	0.04	90.0	100.0
Middle East [e]	4	80.0	0.5	20.0	100.0
8. Sales to home market (percent)					
Latin America	77	5.4	4.0	0.0	100.0
Asia	35	0.1*	6.2	0.0	4.0
Africa	7	0.0*	0.0	0.0	0.0
Middle East [e]	4	0.0*	0.0	0.0	0.0

Table 5 *(continued)*

Characteristic[a]	Number of Observations[b]	Mean	Coefficient of Variation[c]	Range Low	High
9. Locals, management (percent)					
Latin America	77	88.6	0.2	33.0	100.0
Asia	35	78.6*	0.3	0.0	100.0
Africa	8	69.3	0.5	17.0	99.0
Middle East	5	71.4	0.6	0.0	99.0

Note: The findings for each regional group (e.g., Latin America) were computed for each characteristic using all available data.

[a] See Table 2 for description of each characteristic.

[b] See Table 3, note b, for definition.

[c] See Table 3, note c, for definition.

[d] Through the use of t-statistics, the significance of the difference between the means of two sample sets can be tested. This is done by comparing the difference between the means with a measure of the variation from the mean within each sample set. This procedure takes into account the size of the samples in determining the significance of differences between the means. Because the purpose is simply to illustrate the types of analysis that can be done, the mean values of one group of affiliates (the Latin American affiliates) have been taken as the base, and the means of the remaining groups have been compared with them. Latin American affiliates were selected as the base because they are the largest group of subsidiaries. Similar comparisons of other pairs of means can be made by using other bases.

* Probability of significant differences in group means is 90 percent.

** Probability of significant differences in group means is 99 percent.

[c] The figures for the Middle East do *not* include any subsidiaries of petroleum companies.

Finally, local nationals make up a significantly smaller share of management in Asian subsidiaries, compared with their share in Latin American affiliates (Table 5, line 9). Local nationals, on average, constitute 78.6 percent of management in the former and 88.6 percent in the latter. Although the mean percentages of both African and Middle Eastern affiliates are even smaller (69.3 and 71.4 percent, respectively), the differences from the mean of Latin American subsidiaries are not significant.

Index

Acquisition. *See* Takeovers
Adela Investment Co., S.A., 134
Affiliates, statistical profile of, 180–94
Africa, 17, 69, 87, 117, 123, 192–94
Agriculture, 105
Andean Pact countries, 58, 59, 142
Angola, 130
Antitrust legislation, 123, 152, 160; international code for, 140–41
Argentina, 83, 112
Asia, 16, 87, 95, 192–94
Association of Southeast Asian Nations (ASEAN), 142
Australia, 4, 9, 12, 75; participating companies in, 165
Australian firms, 4, 51, 52, 54, 59, 62, 63, 66, 71, 75, 79, 85, 90, 95, 102, 116, 121, 131, 142
Automotive industry, 45, 54–55, 89

Balance of payments, 30, 49, 61, 103, 114, 155
Banks, 45, 55, 60, 93, 107, 132, 133; local borrowing and, 62, 64; takeovers and, 71
Bargaining, 27, 28, 156; host-country–transnational relationships and, 35–36
Belgium, 4, 182; participating company in, 165
Bonds, 132, 134, 160
Borrowing, 34, 160; local, 60–64, 149. *See also* Loans

Brazil, 12, 17, 23, 27, 36, 40, 81, 83, 90, 105; exports and, 105
British firms, 4, 42, 44, 45, 52, 53–54, 59, 62, 63, 66, 67, 71, 74, 75, 77, 78, 81, 84, 85, 87, 90, 99, 101, 104, 108, 110, 112, 116, 119, 125, 126, 128, 135, 137, 142, 157, 159. *See also* United Kingdom

Calvo Doctrine, 105–8, 145–46
Capital, 34, 77; development and, 2; financial transfers and, 132–35; flows of, investment and, 11–12, 22, 23, 24, 29
Chile, 107, 112, 125
Codes: antitrust, 140–41; of conduct, 126–27, 143, 159; disputes and, 161; German tax, 99; for multinationals, 133–37, 160; tax, 118
Colombia, 40
Committee for Economic Development (CED), 1, 4, 7
Compensation (expropriated property), 127–29
Consumption patterns, 32, 47, 73, 151
Corruption, 112, 123, 124–27, 159
Cuba, 124
Currency, 9–11, 12, 16, 23, 28, 61, 62–63, 64, 121

Deferral of taxes. *See* Taxes, deferral
Deterrents to investment, 111–12; instability as, 25–29

195

About the Author

Isaiah Frank is William L. Clayton Professor of International Economics at The Johns Hopkins University School of Advanced International Studies. Prior to joining the Hopkins faculty in 1963, Dr. Frank was Deputy Assistant Secretary of State for Economic Affairs.

Dr. Frank received his Ph.D. in economics from Columbia University, taught economics at Amherst College, and was a Carnegie Fellow at the National Bureau of Economic Research.

Following a wartime assignment in the Office of Strategic Services, Dr. Frank joined the State Department in 1945, where he was, successively, Director of the Office of International Trade Policy and Director of the Office of International Financial and Development Affairs before his appointment as Deputy Assistant Secretary. He also served as a member of President Kennedy's Task Force on Foreign Economic Assistance.

Dr. Frank has played a key role in the development of many aspects of U.S. foreign economic policy and has represented the United States on missions and at conferences in many parts of the world. In recognition of his distinguished contributions to the government, he received the Rockefeller Public Service Award in 1959.

In addition to serving as advisor to various private organizations, including the Committee for Economic Development, Dr. Frank has been a consultant to the World Bank, the United Nations, the Institute for Latin American Integration, the U.S. Treasury Department, the Department of State, and the Agency for International Development.

While on leave from Johns Hopkins in 1970–71, Dr. Frank served as Executive Director of the President's Commission on International Trade and Investment Policy. Since 1975, he has been Chairman of the State Department Advisory Committee on International Investment, Technology, and Development.

Dr. Frank is a frequent contributor to professional journals and is the author of *The European Common Market: An Analysis of Commercial Policy*, coauthor and editor of *The Japanese Economy in International Perspective*, and coauthor of *The Implications of Managed Floating Exchange Rates for U.S. Trade Policy*.